Linguistic Development Through Poetry Memorization

A Mastery Learning Approach

By
Andrew Pudewa

First Edition, 2005
Institute for Excellence in Writing, L.L.C.

Also by Andrew Pudewa:

Advanced Communication Series	*Speech Boot Camp*
Advanced Spelling and Vocabulary	*Student Writing Intensive (Levels A, B, & C)*
Bible-Based Writing Lessons	*Student Intensive Continuation Course (Levels A, B, & C)*
High School Essay Intensive	*Teaching Writing: Structure & Style*
Phonetic Zoo Spelling Program (Levels A, B, & C)	*The Two Andrews: On Writing and Teaching Writing*
The Profound Effects of Music on Life	

Copyright Policy

Linguistic Development Through Poetry Memorization
A Mastery Learning Approach
First Edition, 2005
Second Printing, January 2012
Concept, Presentation, and Commentary © 2005 Andrew Pudewa

ISBN: 978-0-9801005-8-7

Our duplicating/copying policy for this **Teacher's Manual**:

All rights reserved.

No part of this book, or the accompanying disc media, may be reproduced, stored in a retrieval system, or transmitted in any form or by any means, electronic, mechanical, photocopying, recording, or otherwise, without the prior written permission of the author, except as provided by U.S.A. copyright law and the specific policy below:

Home use: You may copy student-related material from this Teacher's Manual for use by multiple children within your immediate family. Disc media may not be copied, except for use within your immediate family.

Small group or co-op classes: Each teacher and participating family is required to purchase a Teacher's Manual. Disc media may not be copied.

Classroom teachers: A Teacher's Manual must be purchased for each teacher. No part of this book may be copied, with the exception of the charts on pages 13-19. Disc media may not be copied.

Library use: Printed materials and disc media may be checked out of a lending library provided patrons agree not to make copies.

Poems that are not in the public domain have been reprinted herein under agreement and/or given proper permissions.

"Stopping by Woods on a Snowy Evening" from THE POETRY OF ROBERT FROST edited by Edward Connery Lathem.
Copyright 1923, 1969 by Henry Holt and Company. Copyright 1951 by Robert Frost.
Reprinted by permission of Henry Holt and Company, L.L.C.

Institute for Excellence in Writing
8799 N. 387 Road
Locust Grove, OK 74352
800.856.5815
info@excellenceinwriting.com
excellenceinwriting.com

Printed in the United States of America

Acknowledgements

Many thanks to all who assisted in the concept and creation of this program, especially:

Harold Pudewa and Marcia McCarry, whose excellent parenting gave me a love for poetry and aptitude with language, enabling me to do the work I do today.

My wife Robin Pudewa and all my children, whose enthusiasm for this project gave me the confidence and energy to see it to completion.

Maria Gerber, Lori Brians, Peter Buscemi, Genevieve Pudewa, and several others, whose research, input, and careful editing contributed greatly to the finished product.

Michael Rabb, a talented homeschooled musician, who graciously provided the piano chimes for the audio recordings.

The many teachers, parents, and students who listened in seminars and lectures as I worked out the concept for this program.

Contents

Prerequisites for Effective Communication	1
Why Memorization?	2
Why Poetry?	4
Mastery Learning—What is it?	6
How This Poetry Memorization Program Is Set Up	9
How to Teach the Program	10
Charts, Record-keeping, and Certificates	12
Level One Poems	21
Level Two Poems	31
Level Three Poems	45
Level Four Poems	61
Level Five: Speech and Soliloquy Suggestions	75
Poet Biographies	77
Bibliography of Anthologies	83

Prerequisites for Effective Communication

As I have traveled the country during the past ten years, working with homeschool students and their parents as well as with teachers and administrators in public and private schools, it has been most gratifying to be able to share an approach to teaching writing that has significantly helped raise the written and oral communication skills of countless children of all ages. The many effective methods and techniques of the *Blended Structure and Style* syllabus, which we use to teach composition, have made a huge difference in the lives of thousands of students, parents, and teachers. However, no matter how brilliant and effective at teaching writing one may become, a frighteningly true and significant fact keeps raising its ugly head. It's simple; it's obvious; it's terribly important, and that is this: **You can't get something out of a child's brain that isn't in there to begin with.**

If you have no Chinese in your brain, you can't get any Chinese out of your brain; if you don't have any music in your brain, you can't get any music out; if you don't have any geometry in, you won't get it out, etc., and this is just as true for one's native language as it is for less familiar subject matter. Getting something into the brain is clearly a prerequisite to getting it out. Now, to be a competent writer or speaker of English, a student need not be well equipped with an extensive knowledge of grammar, nor is it necessary for him to do great loads of worksheets and exercises designed to teach usage and mechanics. It is not necessarily even true that the more time spent writing, the better writer he becomes. If he is a native speaker of English, he needs one thing above all else, and that is this: **a large database in his brain of reliably correct and sophisticated language patterns.**

Reliably correct and sophisticated language patterns are the core of linguistic competence, especially in English, where the "rules" of grammar are less than perfectly consistent, and usages vary greatly because of the uniquely rich multi-lingual origins of the English language. Vocabulary, of course, is critical—but even more vital than knowing a lot of words is knowing how those words naturally, correctly, even artistically fit together in phrases and clauses. The students who write well are always the ones who possess an extensive repertoire of words, an intuitive understanding of when and how those words can be used in idioms and combinations, and an automatic sense of when they have been used correctly or awkwardly. What enables this type of sophisticated linguistic talent is not a conscious knowledge of "rules", but the database of language information that has been stored in the brain.

This brings us to the next question—where do students acquire their database of linguistic patterns? What is the main source of language in children's lives? Although it certainly varies from family to family, for most of the children in this country today the top two sources of linguistic input would likely be the media (TV, radio, Internet, billboards, magazines, and newspapers), and peers (children of approximately the same age). Sadly, as is obvious to any intelligent observer of our culture, neither media nor peers are likely to be a consistent source of what children most need: reliably correct and sophisticated language patterns. Other sources of language in children's lives would be adults—primarily parents and teachers (most of whom are very busy and find that even their communication with children often leans more toward the expedient than toward the sophisticated), and lastly: the books that children read or that adults read out loud to them. Much can be said about why children need to be read to aloud—in much larger quantity than they usually get, even—or especially after they reach an age of being able to read by themselves. However, there is another vital but oft-neglected source of powerful and sophisticated linguistic patterning available to children: memorized language, especially memorized poetry.

WHY MEMORIZATION?

Memorized (or "by heart") language was a mainstay of education for almost all of recorded history until about 60 years ago, when misguided educationists began to promulgate the idea that memorization, along with other types of "rote" learning, was harmful to children's creativity, understanding, and enjoyment of learning. Perhaps one of the most damaging doctrines ever to invade teachers' colleges, the concept that memorization was at best unnecessary and at worst downright harmful, is now handicapping a third generation of students, who, because of the sad state of the popular media, are most in need of the linguistic foundation that memorization provides. It is not uncommon to meet a young teacher or parent who has never even heard of the idea of having children memorize poems or speeches. If they didn't do it as a child, and no one has taught them it would be possible (let alone beneficial), it wouldn't necessarily occur to them. And yet the cultural, neurological, and linguistic value of memorized language is indisputable.

Young children will naturally memorize language patterns from their cultural environment. If teachers and parents don't provide high quality models, kids will automatically internalize and memorize random stuff from their environment—mainly TV advertisements and songs on the radio, most of which we would not find to be "reliably correct and sophisticated." A child's instinctive desire to memorize is intrinsic to language acquisition, yet for the most part we ignore it, or allow it to happen so haphazardly that we miss out on one of the greatest opportunities to build sophisticated language patterns. Poetry has long served a critical role in the transmission of culture, as it tends to convey the "rhyme and reason" of life in a concentrated and memorable form. But if we don't provide the content and opportunity for organized memorization, kids will let popular culture be their teacher. In other words, if we don't provide them with Belloc, Stevenson and Rossetti, they'll memorize McDonald's commercials and Snoop Doggy Dogg rap lines. Memorization is not only natural for young children; it is culturally powerful and educationally essential.

Neurologically, memorization develops the brain in a way nothing else can. Neurons make connections through frequency, intensity, and duration of stimulation.[i] When children memorize (and maintain the ability to recite) interesting poems, all three of these variables are involved in a powerful way, strengthening the network of neural connections that build the foundation of raw intelligence. In short, the more neurons we have connected to other neurons, the more "RAM" we have in the CPU of our brains, and the rigor of memorization is a powerful tool in this process.[ii] Not only is organized memorization important for neurological growth, it also builds a mental discipline that will carry over into other academic areas.

Many of us may know one or more poems, rhymes, or songs from childhood, and we often take some measure of pride or pleasure in being able to recite them to this day. Frequently, the sense of accomplishment that accompanies the memorization of poetry builds linguistic and even academic confidence and spills over into other areas. Like performing a piece of music, memorization and artistic recitation of poetry requires a certain level of perfection, which only conscientious effort and consistency can bring. If a student memorizes a long poem and can recite it flawlessly, he will believe that he can learn anything, be it math processes or facts from history. "By heart" learning not only strengthens the mind, it also strengthens the heart and spirit of the child.

Like any skill, memorization gets easier with practice. Again, as with music, one's first efforts to exactly remember every word in a poem may seem labored and difficult, but as the number of memorized poems increases, so does the ease of mastering new ones. The neural network that stores language grows, and as it does, so does the speed with which new networks of brain cells can be developed and integrated. Retention is also critical. If memorized material is not regularly reviewed and strengthened, it will be lost, and the original neural connections will begin to dissipate. Therefore, critical to the development of any skill, and especially memorization, is the all-important maintenance plan, to assure that what one has worked so hard to attain is not lost by attrition. The more you have learned, the easier it is to learn more. The implications of this fact stretch far beyond the value of just knowing a few dozen poems, but indicate that memory in general can be improved from exercise—just like muscles.

It is sad but true: memorization in schools has for the most part been left by the wayside, thought to be at best unnecessary and at worst harmful. So we now see a third generation of children who will likely be deprived of the many advantages of memorization—not just the neurological ones, but the benefits to heart and mind as well. Whereas students of yesteryear had the common experience of committing to memory a wide range of sophisticated poetry, prose, scripture, and great speeches, children of today often lack exposure to the most common nursery rhymes. Society will not likely notice the serious consequences of this omission until it is too late. Popular culture will continue to dictate the drivel that provides the linguistic and intellectual patterning for a generation, and we will wonder why the schools failed to produce a majority of people who can think and communicate well enough to sustain a free republic.

Why Poetry?

Acknowledging that memorization in general—and memorization of sophisticated language in particular—is a good thing, we must next ask: what should be memorized? Rote learning and recitation of sacred texts has always been a fundamental part of religious education in all major religions from ancient times to the present day, and certainly parents and teachers who raise children to learn large chunks of scripture by heart are persuaded of its spiritual value. Clearly, memorization of classics served as the educational backbone for such thinkers as Aristotle, Saul of Tarsus, Augustine, Thomas Paine, and even more modern authors such as Gene Stratton-Porter and J.R.R. Tolkien. However, poetry has always held a unique position within scripture, classics, and literature for several reasons. Poetry is generally enjoyable, poetry can usually be remembered easily, and good poetry is concentrated—rich in meaning, sophisticated in vocabulary, and solid in structure.

Young children are naturally drawn to humorous, silly, interesting, or unusual things, and many wonderful poems have been written specifically to appeal to children—for good reason. Poets like Hilaire Belloc and Robert Louis Stevenson in the past, or Shel Silverstein and Jack Prelutsky in the present time, have all known how important it is to capture the child's interest in poetry at a young age, thereby preparing them to appreciate more serious and meaningful poems in later years. If children grow up laughing and loving poems, they are much more likely to mature into adults who can pursue and enjoy the classics. When exposure to poetry is limited, or early experience of poetry tedious, students will be unlikely to later benefit from the deeper historical, philosophical, or religious works. *The Psalms, The Bhagavad-Gita, The Odyssey,* and *The Sonnets of Shakespeare* are all poetry in their own right (and even more so in their respective languages), but people won't appreciate their richness without appropriate orientation and experience. As John Senior explained how children must read the "thousand good books" so that as adults they can appreciate the hundred Great Books,[iii] similarly children need broad experience with funny, enjoyable, and dramatic poems so that they can later plumb the minds and hearts of the masters.

Poems by their very nature are easier to remember than prose. This is fortunate. Like songs, the rhyming and rhythmic patterns intrinsic to English poetry create a "predictableness" that aids and speeds memorization. Nursery rhymes exist for a reason. As children internalize those simple patterns, they are preparing for the next level of sophistication. Additionally, rhyming words help build phonetic awareness which strengthens spelling and pronunciation: "Jill/hill" and "down/crown" are simple examples. English rhymes, possible in part because of the vastness of our vocabulary, are pleasant to the ear and to the heart. Alliteration or assonance will accentuate a statement. A solid meter is musical and engaging. Generally, we respond with joy to poetic technique simply because it is artistic, reflecting a higher intelligence, and we are drawn naturally and easily to remember it. Poems are perfect for memorization.

Because poets need to conform to their chosen rhythm and rhyme, they often need to use sophisticated words and grammatical patterns above our normal exposure or conversational usage. This is linguistic gold. By hearing—and better still by memorizing—a variety of poems, we have access to a richness of vocabulary and syntax we might never master in any other way. Again, think of the simple nursery rhyme:

> *Jack and Jill went up the hill*
> *to fetch a pail of water.*
> *Jack fell down and broke his crown,*
> *and Jill came tumbling after.*

The language here, although seemingly simple, gives a young child some very sophisticated elements to work with. While the first sentence contains two prepositional phrases, the second is not only a compound sentence, but also contains dual verbs. The words "fetch", "crown", and "tumbling", are probably beyond the normal conversational level of the young children who would learn the rhyme, but by learning it they would acquire at least familiarity—if not fluency—with those words. They will also learn (long before they'll hear it) that the rule "never end a sentence in a preposition" isn't really true. Find any good poem and evaluate it for vocabulary and grammatical structure; you'll quickly see that poems are almost always high quality language—even the simple, fun ones. When selecting poems for students to memorize, try to choose those that will provide correct and sophisticated linguistic patterns for the child. (But don't be overly picky about it—kids are flexible enough to survive the occasional run-on, fragment, or made-up word.) Memorizing poetry builds effective linguistic aptitude.

Finally, most poems have richness of meaning; they are concentrated thought. Even simple limericks can give opportunity for questions and reflections. Quality humor requires intelligence. Poems that tell a story often have an unexpected twist or embedded moral, while poems that play with words also play with ideas. Emotional poems can help us understand our own complexity of feelings. We have an English idiom, "It has no rhyme nor reason." The two are intertwined towards truth; we trust the beauty of the rhyme as we trust the logic of the reason. As old as language itself, poetry is a powerful tool for communication. Many teachers who value poetry get excited about giving youngsters the opportunity to write poems, yet the children often lack the breadth of experience needed to do much with it. However, by memorizing poetry, children build up a repertoire not only of vocabulary and grammar, but also of poetical ideas—the stuff from which future poems will be crafted. To focus on writing poetry without memorizing it as well is the equivalent of trying to teach musical composition without having the students learn to perform any classic pieces. The results simply won't be as good. Memorization is the most complete form of internalization, and the best way to intimately know something is to know it so well you can communicate it effectively, fluently, even artistically to another. For depth of feeling, meaning, and beauty, poetry is powerful.

Although memorizing scripture and other forms of prose is certainly admirable, poetry holds a few distinct advantages. Not only is it fun, poetry is easy to learn and leads children to a greater depth of thought and word. Most significantly, it promotes fluency with a wide variety of vocabulary and grammatical patterns, something that cannot easily be extracted from daily conversations, from exposure to popular media, nor even from books that children read by themselves. Poetry has always been a civilizing influence in society—from Ancient Greece and Israel, to Feudal Japan, to Victorian England. Poetry is the apex of literature, and thus the crystallized thought of the human race. By internalizing the best of poetry, we preserve and nurture the best of ourselves.

MASTERY LEARNING—WHAT IS IT?

Mastery learning means just that—learning for complete mastery. In the case of memorization, it means knowing every word and its correct place, and being able to recite it with excellent fluency, speed, pronunciation, and inflection. How then does one coach a child toward such perfection? The best example of how this has been done in the past can be seen in the phenomenal results of the Suzuki Method™. Also known as "Talent Education" or Ability Development, Dr. Shinichi Suzuki's original method was called the "Mother Tongue Method of Education" and was based on his observations about how children learn their native language. Suzuki realized that children as young as six or seven years were able to learn to speak a language easily and fluently, but that adults studying a foreign language could seldom reach such a high level of ability even after ten or twenty years of study. He concluded that not only do children have an amazing aptitude for learning anything, but also that the way they best learn is very different than what takes place in traditional education. By observing how children acquire fluency in their mother tongue, he identified four principles—the pillars of Talent Education: 1) the earliest period, 2) the best teacher, 3) the best environment, and 4) the best method of learning.[iv]

Suzuki noted that children begin learning their native language from the earliest possible age; before birth they begin hearing their mother speak. From birth onward they are hearing, trying to understand, and attempting to imitate the language in their environment. He proposed that the young child absorbs language most easily, which concurs with the observations of Maria Montessori,[v] Glen Doman, and many others. Additionally, Suzuki noticed that young children are able to acquire a nuance of expression in dialect that adults are never able to achieve—no matter how many decades of study and practice. He therefore proposed that whatever you want to teach—be it language, music, art, or mathematics—the younger the child is when instruction begins, the more effective the instruction will be. Until Suzuki began demonstrating his amazing results with children as young as three and four years old, music educators generally held that it was best to wait until the child was mature enough to show some potential talent before investing time and money in music lessons.

Suzuki claimed and later proved that "talent" is not only inborn, but that every child has a sprout of talent which can be nurtured from the youngest possible age if the proper methods are used.

Who teaches a child to speak? They don't go to school (and certainly don't have to take any multiple-choice tests) to learn their native tongue; they learn it one-on-one, most often from their mother. Mothers are superbly well qualified to teach their children to speak their language, as they know what they are teaching, and they have time, patience, and love. Dr. Suzuki realized that when mothers are involved, education is at its best, even going so far as to state, "A nation's prosperity depends on women's strength."[vi] The Suzuki Method of music instruction requires a parent to learn all about playing the violin (or 'cello or piano, etc.) and become the "home teacher," guiding the child's practice each day according to the instructions of the music teacher. Educators today still know that results are better when parents are involved, and home school families have found that in most cases they can easily teach children the basic skills of reading, writing, and arithmetic in a fraction of the time required in a typical classroom setting.

Environment is critical. Anyone who has tried to learn a foreign language as an adult is well aware how much easier it is to gain fluency when living in the country or with people who speak it. The classroom/textbook approach to learning a foreign language is notably ineffective, as can be seen by the millions of adults who have "taken" Spanish or French in high school, but couldn't carry on a conversation with a five-year-old native speaker. Suzuki saw how the environment of children was saturated with language—auditory, visual, even kinesthetic—and determined that creating an intensely musical environment was requisite for effective music education. Thus he promoted the use of recordings, so that children could listen every day to the music they were going to be learning to play. Although some traditional music educators considered this to be "cheating" (claiming that students shouldn't hear the melody before figuring it out from the printed notes), Suzuki knew that young children of three or four years old wouldn't be able to read notes for some time, and that to reach a high level of ability, starting young and saturating the environment with music by way of recordings was essential. Now the results are in—Suzuki's methods have produced all the top musicians in the world; the traditionalists are light-years behind. True ability development requires an environment where the student can be deeply immersed in what he is learning.

The fourth pillar of Talent Education, and perhaps most significant for us, is a correct understanding of the method of skill acquisition, since it is so very different from what most of us experienced in our schooling. Suzuki modeled his pedagogy after the way children gain their language ability—one word at a time, while never ceasing to practice and use the words they've learned so far. When children begin to talk, they will begin with one word—usually "mama", and then use that word constantly, even incessantly for everything they want, until using that word has become very easy. That may take days or weeks, but when using that one word has become easy, they will add another word and then use those two words—constantly—until using two words has become easy. That may take days or weeks, but when both of those words can be used easily, fluently, effortlessly, the child will add another, and when using three words is easy they add a fourth, etc., but never stopping the use of the words they have acquired so far. This process continues naturally until by the age of six or seven, an average child has a vocabulary of many thousands of words, which can be combined into phrases, clauses, and sentences, and they do so effortlessly, easily, fluently—to a degree that no one else can do it. Suzuki applied this system to music education, and it is particularly needed in the arts, but the truth of the basic concept is what allows mastery learning in any area of study. We don't, however, truly realize the brilliance of the method until we juxtapose it against our standard textbook-style approach, or what one might call the "non-ability development" method of education.

In a typical school setting, subjects such as history, science, and grammar are generally divided into units and chapters, sections and lists, presented to the students by way of text and lecture/discussion, possibly enhanced with an occasional written paper or project, and finally testing. Once the unit is complete, the curriculum moves on, seldom addressing that chapter's content again (although in high school and college courses, there may be a mid-term or final exam) and it is sooner or later forgotten, until it comes again with the next round of history or science or grammar years later. You probably remember the "chapter test" and how you could cram for that quiz by holding a few dozen miscellaneous facts in your head for a short time—long enough to pass the test—and then safely forget most of it. Overall, retention was poor; lasting benefit was minimal. Unless those bits of information were amazingly interesting to you, there simply wasn't enough frequency, intensity, or duration to allow for permanent retention.

This can be painfully apparent to parents on a daily basis, as evidenced by a child's response to the question, "What did you do in school today?" to which they answer, "Nothing" or "I don't know." This also becomes very clear at the end of the year, when the only thing they remember from seventh grade is the very last chapter of the textbook or the last unit done in science. Typical spelling tests as we may have experienced them are another stunning example of non-ability development education; you get the list on Monday, the pre-test on Wednesday or Thursday, the final test on Friday, and whether a student gets 100% or 80% or 60% on the final, they get a new list on Monday. Repeat. Mastery learning would require the student to score 100%, probably twice in a row, before moving on to a new list—but that would require individualized instruction, which is so very difficult in a classroom setting. Certainly there are exceptions—students who learn and remember more easily, and teachers who cleverly engage students in more effective ways of learning—but they are uncommon. Sad but true: this "non-ability development" method of education is so prevalent today, that we have essentially institutionalized it in universities, where courses are taken mainly for requirements, credits, and grades, and students don't really expect to remember much after the final is passed and the semester is over.

Shinichi Suzuki proved through music education that every child can learn, and that how well they learn can be accelerated by starting at a young age, having the best environment, being coached by the best teacher, and most significantly, using the best method of skills acquisition. When children are taught by good Suzuki Method teachers, they don't stop playing a piece of music just because they've memorized it and are now learning a new piece, no—they play every piece they've learned every day until playing it is easy, effortless, and pretty much perfect. Even then they continue to review regularly, so that they never forget a piece they've learned. That's how—at the age of five or six or seven—a properly trained Suzuki student can perform—nonstop and probably without error—a dozen or more pieces for a Book One graduation recital, making it look simple, easy and fun—an achievement few adults could even imagine. This is true ability development. This is Talent Education. This is mastery learning.

How This Poetry Memorization Program Is Set Up

By now, you should be convinced that memorization helps to grow the brain, build mental discipline, and strengthen the spirit; that poetry is enjoyable, easy to memorize and linguistically rich, and that a high level of ability can be developed by using the Talent Education methodology. If so, you are ready to begin a long-term program to have your students memorize many dozens of poems, be able to recite them with confidence and artistry, and retain that ability for life. The primary benefits will include giving the student not only a rich database of vocabulary and sophisticated English language patterns, but also enhanced memory and intelligence, a greater appreciation for poetry, and even an increased aptitude for writing poems.

Completing this program will likely take several years, but dramatic results should become apparent in just a few months. The method is very similar to Dr. Suzuki's plan for music instruction, with poems divided into four books, or levels. Audio recordings of the poems are included to provide easy opportunity for abundant repetition, which will also allow young children to memorize poems long before they can read them. Level One begins with very short, enjoyable verses. Gradually the length and sophistication of the poems increases. Interspersed throughout all the levels are occasional short selections, so as to give the students a break from too many long ones in a row.

It is recommended that all students, regardless of age, begin with Level One, and proceed through the levels in order. If older students balk at learning some of the simpler or sillier poems, point out to them that such poems will be very handy for entertaining young children they may come across when babysitting, at family gatherings, community events, etc. They may already be teaching younger kids in some capacity, and certainly many will become parents. Poems in this program were chosen with several criteria: humor and enjoyment, vocabulary and linguistic quality, classic and cultural literacy, character and message. The accompanying CDs and charts were designed to help you be successful using the poems in this book; however, if you disapprove of one or more of these selections, you are certainly welcome to replace them with other poems of your own choosing.

Although this compilation contains no distinctly religious content (and is therefore acceptable for purchase and use by public school programs), individual parents or teachers may wish to supplement this compendium with poetry or prose from scriptural or sacred sources of their choice. To that end, we have included space for a few "Personal Selections" at the end of each level. This personal selection requirement will also encourage children in the same family or classroom to individualize the program by choosing a few poems that they especially like.

How to Teach the Program

The basic principle is this: teacher and students recite together one poem several times a day. If the students are able to read, they may have a copy of the poem to follow, if not, then the teacher may need to recite and have students repeat one line at a time. This should be done every school day until the poem can be recited correctly, easily, and without hesitation. (As the first several poems in Level One are quite short, this should happen quickly—perhaps in a few days.) When the first poem is mastered, the second poem is introduced in the same appropriate way, and practiced together several times each day. However, the first poem should not be forgotten; it should also be said at least once each day. When the first two can be easily recited, a third is introduced and practiced, while the first two continue to be recited, and so on. This is the "E.P.E.D." (Every Poem Every Day) method of practice, so that by the end of Level One, the student is reciting every poem they've learned every day. Note: Multi-stanza poems should be learned in sections, with one stanza solidly learned before adding another. It is also preferable that students recite the title and author's name as well.

Some of the poems, especially the older ones, may contain words or idiomatic expressions unfamiliar to students. Additionally, you may find terms or statements of social, scientific, or historical significance. A good teacher will seize the opportunity to explore these words and meanings. Don't assume students have a certain level of understanding. Constantly check for comprehension, and take whatever time is necessary to ensure that students get full value and benefit from the words they are memorizing. Likewise, short biographical statements about the authors have been included when possible, and it is beneficial for students to have some information about the poets whose names they hear and recite. Share this information with them as is appropriate to their age and interest, and do more research together as opportunities arise.

When the student has learned all the poems and is prepared, a Level One graduation party can be scheduled, where family and close friends gather and listen as the student recites, clearly and correctly, all twenty poems of Level One. This event should be accompanied by the presentation of a certificate (and a small party of sorts—perhaps with popcorn and a movie). The student has then graduated to Level Two and now begins to learn the next twenty poems. However, the Level One poems learned must not be forgotten, so the student continues to recite them according to the "E.O.P.E.O.D." (Every Other Poem Every Other Day) schedule while using the "E.P.E.D." schedule for the Level Two poems as they are learned. When ready, the student may do a Level Two Graduation recitation and party, at which point they begin to learn the poems in Level Three. Level One poems are then said according to the "E.T.P.E.T.D" (Every Third Poem Every Third Day) schedule, and Level Two Poems go on the "E.O.P.E.O.D." schedule. This sounds more confusing than it is, but recitation charts are provided to help you and your students stay organized.

By following this method and continuing to regularly recite all the poems learned through to the end of Level Four, students will very likely have achieved a level of frequency, intensity, and duration that will give them life-long retention of all eighty poems—a gift for which they will always be grateful. At some point in the sequence, you may determine to cut back on the E.P.E.D./E.O.P.E.O.D system (perhaps because of time constraints) but you should be certain to provide enough opportunity for recitation of learned poems to maintain the repertoire.

Although memorizing and reciting daily so many poems may at first seem like a daunting project that will require large amounts of time, consider a few points: 1) Given the huge benefits of memorizing poetry, it may well be one of the best uses of your available school hours. 2) Recitation of memorized poems can easily be done away from a desk—perhaps in the car, while cooking or folding clothes, during a walk, etc. 3) Memorizing new poems gets easier in direct proportion to the number of poems already memorized; in other words the more you have learned, the faster you can learn more. 4) The audio CD recordings will help you use repetition so that students can memorize poems more quickly and accurately; you don't have to do it all yourself. So, although it may seem like a huge undertaking, give this system a try, and read the introduction to this book as often as needed to be reminded of the importance of memorizing poetry.

Please note it is very possible that when children memorize and recite poems on a regular basis they may from time to time fall into a "mechanical" or seemingly inappropriate attitude about recitation—either by speaking very fast, getting silly, or simply trying to rush through the poems. This is really not a problem. The goal is to maintain the memorized repertoire; a dramatic recitation each time is not expected. During a Level Graduation event, however, the poems should be "performed" with sufficient volume, clarity, locution, and feeling as possible, and students will likely be inclined to practice in preparation for this.

Lastly, keep in touch. Let us know how it's going—any joys, frustrations, confusions, or problems you may have with this program. I firmly believe that our task of raising leaders, competent communicators who are empowered to speak the truth and speak it well, is an undertaking of monumental importance. Doing our best as parents and teachers, we can perhaps raise up such a generation; let us work together. So don't hesitate to contact me personally if I can be of assistance to you as you strive to prepare your children to write and speak powerfully. May your efforts be blessed and multiplied.

Andrew Pudewa
March 1, 2005

NOTES

[i] Doman, Glenn, and Janet Doman, *How To Multiply Your Baby's Intelligence.* (Philadelphia: Gentle Revolution Press, 2001)

[ii] It is notable that of those who score highest on standardized tests like the SAT, a large number are music and drama students. Although this may be because smart kids are attracted to music and drama (or possibly because these activities are often indicative of a higher economic or social background), it is much more likely due to the fact that music and drama help to create intelligence; both disciplines require large quantities of memorized repertoire.

[iii] Senior, John, *The Restoration of Christian Culture.* (San Francisco: Ignatius Press, 1983)

[iv] Suzuki, Shinichi, *Nurtured by Love* (Tokyo: Suzuki Method International, 1986)

[v] Montessori, Maria, *The Absorbent Mind* (NY: Owl Books, 1995)

[vi] Suzuki, Shinichi, *Young Children's Talent Education & Its Method* (New York: Birch Tree Group, 1999)

CHARTS, RECORD-KEEPING, AND CERTIFICATES

The following six pages are provided to help you organize the E.P.E.D. (Every Poem Every Day), E.O.P.E.O.D. (Every Other Poem Every Other Day) and the E.T.P.E.T.D. (Every Third Poem Every Third Day) systems as described on pages 10-11. Although you may easily be able to do this without such detailed record-keeping, marking the boxes allows children to see their progress and it would be reasonable, especially for young children, to earn a small prize for a well filled in chart. Level One charts are provided for your convenience and to help illustrate the system; the blank charts can be used for Levels Two, Three, and Four. The charts in this book may be copied freely.

Also provided is a sample certificate, which may be used to acknowledge children's progress when they accomplish the perfect memorization of one entire level of twenty poems. Feel free to use it as is, or create your own, more colorful design.

Record Chart One
Every Poem Every Day

Level: __ONE__ Month: _____

#	Title	1	2	3	4	5	6	7	8	9	10	11	12	13	14	15	16	17	18	19	20	21	22	23	24	25	26	27	28	29	30	31
1	Ooey Gooey																															
2	Celery																															
3	The Little Man Who....																															
4	The Vulture																															
5	After the Party																															
6	Singing Time																															
7	The Yak																															
8	The Ingenious Little Old Man																															
9	My Shadow																															
10	There Was an Old Person...																															
11	Jonathan Bing																															
12	Whole Duty of Children																															
13	Godfrey Gordon Gustavus...																															
14	My Gift																															
15	The Swing																															
16	Persevere																															
17	Who Has Seen the Wind?																															
18	The Eagle																															
19	The Swan and the Goose																															
20																																

Record Chart One
Every Poem Every Day

Level: _____   Month: _____

#	Title	1	2	3	4	5	6	7	8	9	10	11	12	13	14	15	16	17	18	19	20	21	22	23	24	25	26	27	28	29	30	31
1																																
2																																
3																																
4																																
5																																
6																																
7																																
8																																
9																																
10																																
11																																
12																																
13																																
14																																
15																																
16																																
17																																
18																																
19																																
20																																

Record Chart One
Every Other Poem Every Other Day

Level: __ONE__ Month: _____

#	Title	1	2	3	4	5	6	7	8	9	10	11	12	13	14	15	16	17	18	19	20	21	22	23	24	25	26	27	28	29	30	31
1	Ooey Gooey																															
2	Celery																															
3	The Little Man Who...																															
4	The Vulture																															
5	After the Party																															
6	Singing Time																															
7	The Yak																															
8	The Ingenious Little Old Man																															
9	My Shadow																															
10	There Was an Old Person...																															
11	Jonathan Bing																															
12	Whole Duty of Children																															
13	Godfrey Gordon Gustavus...																															
14	My Gift																															
15	The Swing																															
16	Persevere																															
17	Who Has Seen the Wind?																															
18	The Eagle																															
19	The Swan and the Goose																															
20																																

Record Chart One
Every Other Poem Every Other Day

Level: _____   Month: _____

#	Title	1	2	3	4	5	6	7	8	9	10	11	12	13	14	15	16	17	18	19	20	21	22	23	24	25	26	27	28	29	30	31
1																																
2																																
3																																
4																																
5																																
6																																
7																																
8																																
9																																
10																																
11																																
12																																
13																																
14																																
15																																
16																																
17																																
18																																
19																																
20																																

Record Chart One
Every Third Poem Every Third Day

Level: **ONE** Month: _____

#	Title	1	2	3	4	5	6	7	8	9	10	11	12	13	14	15	16	17	18	19	20	21	22	23	24	25	26	27	28	29	30	31
1	Ooey Gooey																															
2	Celery																															
3	The Little Man Who...																															
4	The Vulture																															
5	After the Party																															
6	Singing Time																															
7	The Yak																															
8	The Ingenious Little Old Man																															
9	My Shadow																															
10	There Was an Old Person...																															
11	Jonathan Bing																															
12	Whole Duty of Children																															
13	Godfrey Gordon Gustavus...																															
14	My Gift																															
15	The Swing																															
16	Persevere																															
17	Who Has Seen the Wind?																															
18	The Eagle																															
19	The Swan and the Goose																															
20																																

Record Chart One
Every Third Poem Every Third Day

Level: _____   Month: _____

#	Title	1	2	3	4	5	6	7	8	9	10	11	12	13	14	15	16	17	18	19	20	21	22	23	24	25	26	27	28	29	30	31
1																																	
2																																	
3																																	
4																																	
5																																	
6																																	
7																																	
8																																	
9																																	
10																																	
11																																	
12																																	
13																																	
14																																	
15																																	
16																																	
17																																	
18																																	
19																																	
20																																	

Certificate of Completion

THIS CERTIFIES THAT

_____

HAS SUCCESSFULLY COMPLETED THE MEMORIZATION
AND PRESENTATION REQUIREMENTS FOR

LEVEL _____ OF

Linguistic Development Through Poetry Memorization

_____ _____
Date   Supervisor

Level One

Level One Poems

1. **Ooey Gooey** [Author Unknown] — 22
2. **Celery** by Ogden Nash — 22
3. **The Little Man Who Wasn't There** by Hughes Mearns — 22
4. **The Vulture** by Hilaire Belloc — 22
5. **After the Party** by William Wise — 23
6. **Singing Time** by Rose Fyleman — 23
7. **The Yak** by Hilaire Belloc — 24
8. **The Ingenious Little Old Man** by John Bennet — 24
9. **My Shadow** by Robert Louis Stevenson — 25
10. **There Was an Old Person Whose Habits** by Edward Lear — 25
11. **Jonathan Bing** by Beatrice Curtis Brown — 26
12. **Whole Duty of Children** by Robert Louis Stevenson — 26
13. **Godfrey Gordon Gustavus Gore** by William Brighty Rands — 27
14. **My Gift** by Christina Rossetti — 28
15. **The Swing** by Robert Louis Stevenson — 28
16. **Persevere** [Author Unknown] — 28
17. **Who Has Seen the Wind?** by Christina Rossetti — 29
18. **The Eagle** by Alfred Tennyson — 29
19. **The Swan and the Goose** by William Ellery Leonard — 29
20. Personal Selection (8 lines or shorter) — 29

NOTES:

Several versions of "Ooey Gooey" seem to be floating around, and even the spelling of the title is in question. I have chosen the one I like most—but don't be surprised if you come across variations.

After starting Belloc's poem "The Yak", our family enjoyed consulting the encyclopedia and discovering a bit about Yaks; we found that Belloc's statements may not be quite as odd as we first thought.

Edward Lear wrote countless limericks, ranging from the cute to the inane, most of which can be found in his 1846 manuscript, *A Book of Nonsense*. You may (or may not) enjoy reading more of his absurd verses, but either way you'll be amazed and laugh at his drawings.

"Persevere" seems to have first appeared in the McGuffey Readers.

For the Level One Personal Selection, you may enjoy looking into the work of more modern poets such as Shel Silverstein and Jack Prelutsky, who both wrote many books of delightful (and often silly) poems for children. A bibliography of anthologies is provided for you on the last page of this book.

Level One

1. **Ooey Gooey** [Author Unknown]

Ooey Gooey was a worm,
A mighty worm was he.
He stepped upon the railroad tracks,
The train he did not see!
Ooooey Goooey!

2. **Celery** by Ogden Nash

Celery, raw,
Develops the jaw,
But celery, stewed,
Is more quietly chewed.

3. **The Little Man Who Wasn't There** by Hughes Mearns

As I was going up the stair,
I met a man who wasn't there;
He wasn't there again today!
I wish, I *wish,* he'd stay away.

4. **The Vulture** by Hilaire Belloc

The vulture eats between his meals,
And that's the reason why
He very, very rarely feels
As well as you or I.

His eye is dull. His head is bald,
His neck is growing thinner,
Oh, what a lesson for us all,
To only eat at dinner!

Level One

5. **After the Party** by William Wise

Jonathan Blake
Ate too much cake,
He isn't himself today;
He's tucked up in bed
With a feverish head,
And he doesn't much care to play.

Jonathan Blake
Ate too much cake,
And three kinds of ice cream too—
From his latest reports
He's quite out of sorts,
And I'm sure the reports are true.

I'm sorry to state
That he also ate
Six pickles, a pie, and a pear;
In fact I confess
It's a reasonable guess
He ate practically everything there.

Yes, Jonathan Blake
Ate too much cake,
So he's not at his best today;
But there's no need for sorrow—
If you come back tomorrow,
I'm sure he'll be out to play.

6. **Singing Time** by Rose Fyleman

I wake in the morning early
And always, the very first thing,
I poke out my head and I sit up in bed
And I sing and I sing and I sing.

Level One

7. **The Yak** by Hilaire Belloc

As a friend to the children, commend me the Yak;
You will find it exactly the thing;
It will carry and fetch, you can ride on its back,
Or lead it about with a string.

The Tartar who dwells on the plains of Tibet
(A desolate region of snow),
Has for centuries made it a nursery pet,
And surely the Tartar should know!

Then tell your papa where the Yak can be got,
And if he is awfully rich,
He will buy you the creature—or else he will not
(I cannot be positive which).

8. **The Ingenious Little Old Man** by John Bennett

A little old man of the sea
Went out in a boat for a sail:
The water came in
Almost up to his chin
And he had nothing with which to bail.

But this little old man of the sea
Just drew out his jack-knife so stout,
And a hole with its blade
In the bottom he made,
So that all of the water ran out.

Level One

9. **My Shadow** by Robert Louis Stevenson

I have a little shadow that goes in and out with me,
And what can be the use of him is more than I can see.
He is very, very like me from the heels up to the head;
And I see him jump before me, when I jump into my bed.

The funniest thing about him is the way he likes to grow—
Not at all like proper children, which is always very slow;
For he sometimes shoots up taller like an India-rubber ball,
And he sometimes gets so little that there's none of him at all.

He hasn't got a notion of how children ought to play,
And can only make a fool of me in every sort of way.
He stays so close beside me, he's a coward you can see;
I'd think shame to stick to nursie as that shadow sticks to me!

One morning, very early, before the sun was up,
I rose and found the shining dew on every buttercup;
But my lazy little shadow, like an arrant sleepyhead,
Had stayed at home behind me and was fast asleep in bed.

10. **There Was an Old Person Whose Habits** by Edward Lear

There was an Old Person whose habits
Induced him to feed upon rabbits;
When he'd eaten eighteen,
He turned perfectly green
Upon which he relinquished those habits.

Level One

11. **Jonathan Bing** by Beatrice Curtis Brown

Poor old Jonathan Bing
Went out in his carriage to visit the King,
But everyone pointed and said, "Look at that!
Jonathan Bing has forgotten his hat!"
(He'd forgotten his hat!)

Poor old Jonathan Bing
Went home and put on a new hat for the King,
But up by the palace a soldier said, "Hi!
You can't see the King; you've forgotten your tie!"
(He'd forgotten his tie!)

Poor old Jonathan Bing
He put on a *beautiful* tie for the King,
But when he arrived an Archbishop said, "Ho!
You can't come to court in pyjamas, you know!"

Poor old Jonathan Bing
Went home and addressed a short note to the King:
    If you please will excuse me
    I won't come to tea;
    For home's the best place for
    All people like me!

12. **Whole Duty of Children** by Robert Louis Stevenson

A child should always say what's true,
And speak when he is spoken to,
And behave mannerly at table;
At least as far as he is able.

LEVEL ONE

13. **Godfrey Gordon Gustavus Gore** by William Brighty Rands

Godfrey Gordon Gustavus Gore—
No doubt you have heard the name before—
Was a boy who would never shut a door!

The wind might whistle, the wind might roar,
And teeth be aching and throats be sore,
But still he never would shut the door.

His father would beg, his mother implore,
"Godfrey Gordon Gustavus Gore,
We really do wish you would shut the door!"

Their hands they rung, their hair they tore;
But Godfrey Gordon Gustavus Gore
Was deaf as the buoy out at the Nore.

When he walked forth the folks would roar,
"Godfrey Gordon Gustavus Gore,
Why don't you think to shut the door?"

They rigged out a Shutter with sail and oar,
And threatened to pack off Gustavus Gore
On a voyage of penance to Singapore,

But he begged for mercy, and said, "No more!
Pray do not send me to Singapore
On a Shutter, and then I will shut the door!"

"You will?" said his parents; "then keep on shore!
But mind you do! For the plague is sore
Of a fellow that never will shut the door,
Godfrey Gordon Gustavus Gore!"

14. **My Gift*** by Christina Rossetti

What can I give Him
Poor as I am;
If I were a shepherd,
I would give Him a lamb.

If I were a wise man,
I would do my part.
Yet what I can I give Him,
Give my heart.

*Composers have tweaked Rossetti's poem to make the lyric fit their melodies. Different versions appear online.

15. **The Swing** by Robert Louis Stevenson

How do you like to go up in a swing,
    Up in the air so blue?
Oh, I do think it the pleasantest thing
    Ever a child can do!

Up in the air and over the wall,
    'Till I can see so wide,
Rivers and trees and cattle and all
    Over the countryside—

'Till I look down on the garden green,
    Down on the roof so brown—
Up in the air I go flying again,
    Up in the air and down!

16. **Persevere** [Author Unknown]

The fisher who draws in his net too soon,
Won't have any fish to sell;
The child who shuts up his book too soon,
Won't learn any lessons well.

If you would have your learning stay,
Be patient—don't learn too fast;
The man who travels a mile each day,
May get 'round the world at last.

LEVEL ONE

17. **Who Has Seen the Wind?** by Christina Rossetti

Who has seen the wind?
    Neither I nor you:
But when the leaves hang trembling
    The wind is passing through.

Who has seen the wind?
    Neither you nor I:
But when the trees bow down their heads
    The wind is passing by.

18. **The Eagle** by Alfred Tennyson

He clasps the crag with crooked hands;
Close to the sun in lonely lands.
Ringed with the azure world, he stands.

The wrinkled sea beneath him crawls;
He watches from his mountain walls.
And like a thunderbolt he falls.

19. **The Swan and the Goose** by William Ellery Leonard

A rich man bought a Swan and Goose—
That for song, and this for use.
It chanced his simple-minded cook
One night the Swan for Goose mistook.

But in the dark about to chop
The Swan in two above the crop,
He heard the lyric note, and stayed
The action of the fatal blade.
    And thus we see a proper tune
    Is sometimes very opportune.

20. Personal Selection (8 lines or shorter)

Level One

Level Two

Level Two Poems

1.	**How Doth the Little Crocodile** by Lewis Carroll	32
2.	**At the Seaside** by Robert Louis Stevenson	32
3.	**Rebecca, Who Slammed Doors for Fun and Perished Miserably** by Hilaire Belloc	33
4.	**Fog** by Carl Sandburg	34
5.	**Some One** by Walter de la Mare	34
6.	**The Duke of Plaza-Toro** by W.S. Gilbert	35
7.	**God and the Soldier** [Author Unknown]	35
8.	**Jabberwocky** by Lewis Carroll	36
9.	**The Height of the Ridiculous** by Oliver Wendell Holmes	37
10.	**The Spider and the Fly** by Mary Howitt	37
11.	**Trees** by Joyce Kilmer	39
12.	**The Captain's Daughter** by James T. Fields	39
13.	**The Charge of the Light Brigade** by Alfred Tennyson	40
14.	**Sea Fever** by John Masefield	41
15.	**Shoes** by Louis Untermeyer	41
16.	**The Glove and the Lions** by Leigh Hunt	42
17.	**Conscience & Remorse** by Paul Laurence Dunbar	43
18.	**Stopping by Woods on a Snowy Evening** by Robert Frost	43
19.	**Project** by Mary Fabyan Windeatt	44
20.	Personal Selection (12 lines or shorter)	44

NOTES:

You will notice that there are several more "serious" poems in Level Two. Be sure to talk about the poems, defining any unusual words or usages. That said, it is also important to keep in mind that the poem does not have to be fully or perfectly understood to be of great value—even after the hundredth recitation, new insights can occur to a student of any age.

W.S. Gilbert is the Gilbert of Gilbert & Sullivan fame. "The Duke of Plaza-Toro" was originally written for the comedic opera, *The Gondoliers*.

"The Charge of the Light Brigade" documents an actual historical event, which occurred in 1854 during the Crimean War. Major General the Earl of Cardigan led 661 men in a charge against the well-fortified Russian forces. Only 195 men with horses returned.

Kilmer's "Trees" is a famous poem, but not always engaging to children. "Shoes" by Untermeyer is clearly a take-off or parody of "Trees." Children who find the former dull will be quite exited to learn the latter. Ambitious students can be encouraged to do their own "spoof" of a poem they know, trying to imitate the rhyme and meter, but changing the context and words. In truth, there is a long tradition of poets satirizing and mimicking each other.

Level Two

1. **How Doth the Little Crocodile** by Lewis Carroll

How doth the little crocodile
    Improve his shining tail,
And pour the waters of the Nile
    On every golden scale!

How cheerfully he seems to grin,
    How neatly spreads his claws,
And welcomes little fishes in
    With gently smiling jaws!

2. **At the Seaside** by Robert Louis Stevenson

When I was down beside the sea
A wooden spade they gave to me
    To dig the sandy shore.
My holes were empty like a cup.
In every hole the sea came up,
    'Till it could come no more.

3. **Rebecca, Who Slammed Doors for Fun and Perished Miserably**
   by Hilaire Belloc

A trick that everyone abhors
In Little Girls is slamming Doors.
A Wealthy Banker's Little Daughter
Who lived in Palace Green, Bayswater
(By name Rebecca Offendort),
Was given to this Furious Sport.

She would deliberately go
And Slam the door like Billy-Ho!
To make her Uncle Jacob start.
She was not actually bad at heart,
But only rather rude and wild:
She was an aggravating child….

It happened that a Marble Bust
Of Abraham was standing just
Above the Door this little Lamb
Had carefully prepared to Slam,
And Down it came! It knocked her flat!
It laid her out! She looked like that.

Her Funeral Sermon (which was long
And followed by a Sacred Song)
Mentioned her Virtues, it is true,
But dwelt upon her Vices too,
And showed the Dreadful End of One
Who goes and slams the Door for Fun.

The children who were brought to hear
The awful Tale from far and near
Were much impressed, and inly swore
They never more would slam the Door.
—As often they had done before.

Level Two

4. **Fog** by Carl Sandburg

The fog comes
on little cat feet.

It sits looking
over harbor and city
on silent haunches
and then, moves on.

5. **Some One** by Walter de la Mare

Some one came knocking
    At my wee, small door;
Some one came knocking,
    I'm sure—sure—sure;
I listened, I opened,
    I looked to left and right,
But nought there was a-stirring
    In the still dark night.
Only the busy beetle
    Tap-tapping in the wall,
Only from the forest
    The screech-owl's call,
Only the cricket whistling
    While the dewdrops fall,
So I know not who came knocking,
    At all, at all, at all.

6. **The Duke of Plaza-Toro** by W.S. Gilbert

In enterprise of martial kind,
When there was any fighting,
He led his regiment from behind—
He found it less exciting.

But when away his regiment ran,
His place was at the fore, O—
That celebrated,
Cultivated,
Underrated
Nobleman,
The Duke of Plaza-Toro!

In the first and foremost flight, ha, ha!
You always found that knight, ha, ha!
That celebrated,
Cultivated,
Underrated
Nobleman,
The Duke of Plaza-Toro!

When, to evade Destruction's hand,
To hide they all proceeded,
No soldier in that gallant band
Hid half as well as he did.

He lay concealed throughout the war,
And so preserved his gore, O!
That unaffected,
Undetected,
Well-connected
Warrior,
The Duke of Plaza-Toro!

In every doughty deed, ha, ha!
He always took the lead, ha, ha!
That unaffected,
Undetected,
Well-connected
Warrior,
The Duke of Plaza-Toro!

7. **God and the Soldier** [Author Unknown]

God and the Soldier
All men adore
In time of trouble,
And no more;
For when war is over
And all things righted
God is neglected—
The old soldier slighted.

8. **Jabberwocky** by Lewis Carroll

'Twas brillig, and the slithy toves
    Did gyre and gimble in the wabe:
All mimsy were the borogoves,
    And the mome raths outgrabe.

"Beware the Jabberwock, my son!
    The jaws that bite, the claws that catch!
Beware the Jubjub bird, and shun
    The frumious Bandersnatch!"

He took his vorpal sword in hand:
    Long time the manxome foe he sought—
So rested he by the Tumtum tree,
    And stood awhile in thought.

And, as in uffish thought he stood,
    The Jabberwock, with eyes of flame,
Came whiffling through the tulgey wood,
    And burbled as it came!

One, two! One, two! And through and through
    The vorpal blade went snicker-snack!
He left it dead, and with its head
    He went galumphing back.

"And hast thou slain the Jabberwock?
    Come to my arms, my beamish boy!
O frabjous day! Callooh! Callay!"
    He chortled in his joy.

'Twas brillig, and the slithy toves
    Did gyre and gimble in the wabe:
All mimsy were the borogoves,
    And the mome raths outgrabe.

Level Two

9. The Height of the Ridiculous by Oliver Wendell Holmes

I wrote some lines once on a time
In wondrous merry mood,
And thought, as usual, men would say
They were exceeding good.

They were so queer, so very queer,
I laughed as I would die;
Albeit, in the general way,
A sober man am I.

I called my servant, and he came;
How kind it was of him
To mind a slender man like me,
He of the mighty limb.

"These to the printer," I exclaimed,
And, in my humorous way,
I added (as a trifling jest),
"There'll be the devil to pay."

He took the paper, and I watched,
And saw him peep within;
At the first line he read, his face
Was all upon the grin.

He read the next; the grin grew broad,
And shot from ear to ear;
He read the third; a chuckling noise
I now began to hear.

The fourth: he broke into a roar;
The fifth: his waistband split;
The sixth: he burst five buttons off,
And tumbled in a fit.

Ten days and nights, with sleepless eye,
I watched that wretched man,
And since, I never dare to write
As funny as I can.

10. The Spider and the Fly by Mary Howitt

"Will you walk into my parlor?" said the Spider to the Fly,
" 'Tis the prettiest little parlor that ever you did spy;
The way into my parlor is up a winding stair,
And I have many curious things to show when you are there."
"Oh no, no," said the little Fly, "to ask me is in vain;
For who goes up your winding stair can ne'er come down again."

"I'm sure you must be weary, dear, with soaring up so high;
Will you rest upon my little bed?" said the Spider to the Fly.
"There are pretty curtains drawn around, the sheets are fine and thin;
And if you like to rest awhile, I'll snugly tuck you in!"
"Oh no, no," said the little Fly, "for I've often heard it said
They never, never wake again, who sleep upon your bed!"

(Continued on next page)

Level Two

(The Spider and the Fly, continued)

Said the cunning Spider to the Fly, "Dear friend, what can I do
To prove the warm affection I've always felt for you?
I have within my pantry, good store of all that's nice;
I'm sure you're very welcome—will you please to take a slice?"
"Oh no, no," said the little Fly, "kind sir, that cannot be,
I've heard what's in your pantry, and I do not wish to see!"

"Sweet creature," said the Spider, "you're witty and you're wise;
How handsome are your gauzy wings, how brilliant are your eyes!
I have a little looking-glass upon my parlor shelf;
If you'll step in one moment, dear, you shall behold yourself."
"I thank you, gentle sir," she said, "for what you're pleased to say,
And bidding you good-morning now, I'll call another day."

The spider turned him round about, and went into his den,
For well he knew the silly Fly would soon come back again;
So he wove a subtle web in a little corner sly,
And set his table ready to dine upon the Fly.
Then he came out to his door again, and merrily did sing,
"Come hither, hither, pretty Fly, with the pearl and silver wing;
Your robes are green and purple, there's a crest upon your head;
Your eyes are like the diamond bright, but mine are dull as lead."

Alas, alas, how very soon this silly little Fly,
Hearing his wily, flattering words, came slowly flitting by;
With buzzing wings she hung aloft, then near and nearer drew—
Thinking only of her brilliant eyes, and green and purple hue;
Thinking only of her crested head—poor foolish thing! At last,
Up jumped the cunning Spider, and fiercely held her fast.
He dragged her up his winding stair, into his dismal den
Within his little parlor—but she ne'er came out again!

And now, dear little children, who may this story read,
To idle, silly, flattering words, I pray you ne'er give heed;
Unto an evil counselor close heart, and ear, and eye,
And take a lesson from this tale of the Spider and the Fly.

11. **Trees** by Joyce Kilmer

I think that I shall never see
A poem lovely as a tree.
A tree whose hungry mouth is prest
Against the earth's sweet flowing breast;
A tree that looks at God all day,
And lifts her leafy arms to pray;
A tree that may in Summer wear
A nest of robins in her hair;
Upon whose bosom snow has lain;
Who intimately lives with rain.
Poems are made by fools like me,
But only God can make a tree.

12. **The Captain's Daughter** by James T. Fields

We were crowded in the cabin,
    Not a soul would dare to sleep—
It was midnight on the waters,
    And a storm was on the deep.

'Tis a fearful thing in winter
    To be shattered by the blast,
And to hear the rattling trumpet
    Thunder, "Cut away the mast!"

So we shuddered there in silence—
    For the stoutest held his breath,
While the hungry sea was roaring
    And the breakers talked with Death.

As thus we sat in darkness,
    Each one busy with his prayers,
"We are lost!" the captain shouted
    As he staggered down the stairs.

But his little daughter whispered,
    As she took his icy hand,
"Isn't God upon the ocean,
    Just the same as on the land?"

Then we kissed the little maiden,
    And we spoke in better cheer,
And we anchored safe in harbor
    When the morn was shining clear.

Level Two

13. The Charge of the Light Brigade by Alfred, Lord Tennyson

Half a league, half a league,
Half a league onward,
All in the valley of Death
    Rode the six hundred.

"Forward the Light Brigade!
Charge for the guns!" he said.
Into the valley of Death
    Rode the six hundred.

"Forward, the Light Brigade!"
Was there a man dismayed?
Not though the soldier knew
    Some one had blundered.

Theirs not to make reply,
Theirs not to reason why,
Theirs but to do and die.
Into the valley of Death
    Rode the six hundred.

Cannon to right of them,
Cannon to left of them,
Cannon in front of them
    Volleyed and thundered;
Stormed at with shot and shell,
Boldly they rode and well,
Into the jaws of Death,
Into the mouth of Hell
    Rode the six hundred.

Flashed all their sabers bare,
Flashed as they turned in air
Sabring the gunners there,
Charging an army, while
    All the world wondered.

Plunged in the battery-smoke
Right through the line they broke;
Cossack and Russian
Reeled from the sabre-stroke
Shattered and sundered.
Then they rode back, but not,
    Not the six hundred.

Cannon to right of them,
Cannon to left of them,
Cannon behind them
    Volleyed and thundered;
Stormed at with shot and shell,
While horse and hero fell,
They that had fought so well
Came through the jaws of Death,
Back from the mouth of Hell,
All that was left of them,
    Left of six hundred.

When can their glory fade?
Oh, the wild charge they made!
    All the world wondered.
Honor the charge they made!
Honor the Light Brigade,
    Noble six hundred!

Level Two

14. **Sea Fever** by John Masefield

I must go down to the seas again, to the lonely sea and the sky,
And all I ask is a tall ship and a star to steer her by,
And the wheel's kick and the wind's song and the white sail's shaking,
And a gray mist on the sea's face, and a gray dawn breaking.

I must go down to the seas again, for the call of the running tide
Is a wild call and a clear call that may not be denied;
And all I ask is a windy day with the white clouds flying,
And the flung spray and the blown spume, and the sea gulls crying.

I must go down to the seas again, to the vagrant gypsy life,
To the gull's way and the whale's way where the wind's like a whetted knife;
And all I ask is a merry yarn from a laughing fellow-rover,
And quiet sleep and a sweet dream when the long trick's over.

15. **Shoes** by Louis Untermeyer

I think that no one ever knew
A poem lovely as a shoe.

A shoe that has so much of grace,
Tied and adorned with its own lace.

A shoe that will, in winter, wear
Rubbers to skid with everywhere.

A shoe that points to its own goal,
And looks well-heeled to save its sole.

Poems are made by fools like you.
But one old woman lived in a shoe!

16. **The Glove and the Lions** by James Leigh Hunt

King Francis was a hearty king, and loved a royal sport,
And one day, as his lions fought, sat looking on the court;
The nobles filled the benches round, the ladies by their side,
And 'mongst them sat the Count de Lorge, with one for whom he sighed:
And truly 't was a gallant thing to see that crowning show,
Valor and love, and a king above, and the royal beasts below.

Ramped and roared the lions, with horrid laughing jaws;
They bit, they glared, gave blows like beams, a wind went with their paws;
With wallowing might and stifled roar, they rolled on one another:
'Till all the pit, with sand and mane, was in a thunderous smother;
The bloody foam above the bars came whizzing through the air:
Said Francis, then, "Faith, gentlemen, we're better here than there."

De Lorge's love o'erheard the king,–a beauteous, lively dame,
With smiling lips, and sharp, bright eyes, which always seemed the same;
She thought, "The Count, my lover, is brave as brave can be,
He surely would do wondrous things to show his love for me;
King, ladies, lovers, all look on; the occasion is divine;
I'll drop my glove to prove his love; great glory will be mine."

She dropped her glove to prove his love, then looked at him and smiled;
He bowed, and in a moment leaped among the lions wild;
The leap was quick, return was quick, he soon regained his place,
Then threw the glove, but not with love, right in the lady's face.
"In faith," cried Francis, "rightly done!" and he rose from where he sat;
"No love," quoth he, "but vanity, sets love a task like that."

Level Two

17. **Conscience and Remorse** by Paul Laurence Dunbar

"Good-bye," I said to my conscience–
"Good-bye for aye and aye,"
And I put her hands off harshly,
And turned my face away;
And conscience smitten sorely
Returned not from that day.

But a time came when my spirit
Grew weary of its pace;
And I cried: "Come back, my conscience;
I long to see thy face."
But conscience cried; "I cannot;
Remorse sits in my place."

18. **Stopping by Woods on a Snowy Evening** by Robert Frost

Whose woods these are I think I know.
His house is in the village, though;
He will not see me stopping here
To watch his woods fill up with snow.

My little horse must think it queer
To stop without a farmhouse near
Between the woods and frozen lake
The darkest evening of the year.

He gives his harness bells a shake
To ask if there is some mistake.
The only other sound's the sweep
Of easy wind and downy flake.

The woods are lovely, dark, and deep,
But I have promises to keep,
and miles to go before I sleep.
And miles to go before I sleep.

Level Two

19. **Project** by Mary Fabyan Windeatt

Now it is well
That we should start
Planning a Fortress
In the Heart;

Building with things
Which will endure
Longer than Sorrow's
Signature

(Take away stone,
Take away wood;
Faith is ten thousand
Times as good)

Take away steel,
Take away lead;
Charity, hope, will
Do instead!

Thus when the years
Pile up the pain
We can go seeking
Peace again;

Back of the walls
Heaven designed
Just for the hurts of
Humankind.

20. Personal Selection (12 lines or shorter)

Level Three

Level Three

1.	**A Young Lady Named Bright** by Edward Lear	46
2.	**A Psalm of Life** by Henry Wadsworth Longfellow	46
3.	**The Road Not Taken** by Robert Frost	47
4.	**O Captain! My Captain!** by Walt Whitman	47
5.	**Matilda: Who Told Lies, and Was Burned to Death** by Hilaire Belloc	48
6.	**Scintillate, Scintillate, Globule Vivific** by Dave Arns	48
7.	**What I Live For** [Author Unknown]	49
8.	**Courage** by Sister M. Eulalia, RSM	49
9.	**Grandfather's Clock** by Henry Clay Work	50
10.	**The Touch of the Master's Hand** by Myra Brooks Welch	51
11.	**The Unknown Soldier** by Billy Rose	52
12.	**The Pessimist** by Ben King & **The Optimist** [Author Unknown]	53
13.	**The Fool's Prayer** by Edward Roland Sill	54
14.	**Casey at the Bat** by Ernest Lawrence Thayer	54
15.	**He Wishes for the Cloths of Heaven** by W.B. Yeats	56
16.	**The Destruction of Sennacherib** by Lord Byron	56
17.	**The Village Blacksmith** by Henry Wadsworth Longfellow	57
18.	**When I Heard the Learn'd Astronomer** by Walt Whitman	58
19.	**Casey's Revenge** by Grantland Rice	58
20.	Personal Selection (any length)	59

NOTES:

Walt Whitman wrote "O Captain, My Captain!" in response to the assassination of Abraham Lincoln. The country mourned with this metaphor.

Henry Work's "Grandfather's Clock" is perhaps more well-known as a song than a poem; if the student prefers to sing it, that would be fine.

Dave Arns' poem should be recognizable as a "Thesaurusoetry" version of the familiar song (especially to music students). Do a web search for "thesaurusoetry", and you'll find many more versions of this one . . . but Dave did it best!

The story of "The Destruction of Sennacherib" is documented in Second Chronicles, which would be worth reading a few times while learning this poem. Describing this historical and biblical event, the poem emphasizes the sovereign nature of Providence.

"Casey at the Bat" is a classic, while "Casey's Revenge" is a fun sequel worth knowing.

Level Three

1. **A Young Lady Named Bright** by Edward Lear

There was a young lady named Bright,
Who traveled much faster than light.
    She started one day
    In the relative way,
And returned on the previous night.

2. **A Psalm of Life** by Henry Wordsworth Longfellow

Tell me not, in mournful numbers,
Life is but an empty dream!—
For the soul is dead that slumbers,
And things are not what they seem.

Life is real! Life is earnest!
And the grave is not its goal;
Dust thou art, to dust returnest,
Was not spoken of the soul.

Not enjoyment, and not sorrows,
Is our destined end or way;
But to act, that each to-morrow
Find us farther than to-day.

Art is long, and Time is fleeting,
And our hearts, though stout and brave,
Still, like muffled drums, are beating
Funeral marches to the grave.

In the world's broad field of battle,
In the bivouac of Life,
Be not like dumb, driven cattle!
Be a hero in the strife!

Trust no future, howe'er pleasant!
Let the dead Past bury its dead!
Act, —act in the living Present!
Heart within, and God o'erhead!

Lives of great men all remind us
We can make our lives sublime,
And, departing, leave behind us
Footprints on the sands of time;

Footprints, that perhaps another,
Sailing o'er life's solemn main,
A forlorn and shipwrecked brother,
Seeing, shall take heart again.

Let us, then, be up and doing,
With a heart for any fate;
Still achieving, still pursuing,
Learn to labor and to wait.

Level Three

3. The Road Not Taken by Robert Frost

Two roads diverged in a yellow wood,
And sorry I could not travel both
And be one traveler, long I stood
And looked down one as far as I could
To where it bent in the undergrowth;

Then took the other, as just as fair,
And having perhaps the better claim,
Because it was grassy and wanted wear;
Though as for that the passing there
Had worn them really about the same,

And both that morning equally lay
In leaves no step had trodden black.
Oh, I kept the first for another day!
Yet knowing how way leads on to way,
I doubted if I should ever come back.

I shall be telling this with a sigh
Somewhere ages and ages hence;
Two roads diverged in a wood, and I—
I took the one less traveled by,
And that has made all the difference.

4. O Captain! My Captain! by Walt Whitman

O Captain! My Captain! our fearful trip is done,
The ship has weathered every rack, the prize we sought is won,
The port is near, the bells I hear, the people all exulting,
While follow eyes the steady keel, the vessel grim and daring;

    But O heart! heart! heart!
        O the bleeding drops of red,
            Where on the deck my Captain lies,
                Fallen cold and dead.

O Captain! My Captain! rise up and hear the bells;
Rise up—for you the flag is flung—for you the bugle trills,
For you bouquets and ribboned wreaths—for you the shores a-crowding,
For you they call, the swaying mass, their eager faces turning;

    Here Captain! dear father!
        This arm beneath your head!
            It is some dream that on the deck
                You've fallen cold and dead.

My Captain does not answer, his lips are pale and still,
My father does not feel my arm, he has no pulse nor will,
The ship is anchored safe and sound, its voyage closed and done,
From fearful trip the victor ship comes in with object won;

    Exult O shores, and ring O bells!
        But I, with mournful tread,
            Walk the deck my Captain lies,
                Fallen cold and dead.

LEVEL THREE

5. **Matilda: Who Told Lies, and Was Burned to Death** by Hilaire Belloc

Matilda told such Dreadful Lies,
It made one Gasp and Stretch one's Eyes;
Her Aunt, who, from her Earliest Youth,
Had kept a Strict Regard for Truth,
Attempted to believe Matilda:
The effort very nearly killed her,
And would have done so, had not She
Discovered this Infirmity.

For once, towards the Close of Day,
Matilda, growing tired of play,
And finding she was left alone,
Went tiptoe to the Telephone
And summoned the Immediate Aid
Of London's Noble Fire-Brigade.

Within an hour the gallant Band
Were pouring in on every hand,
From Putney, Hackney Downs, and Bow
With Courage high and Hearts a-glow
They galloped, roaring through the Town,
"Matilda's House is Burning Down!"
Inspired by British Cheers and Loud
Proceeding from the Crowd,

They ran their ladders through a Score
Of windows on the Ball Room Floor;
And took Peculiar Pains to Souse
The Pictures up and down the House,
Until Matilda's Aunt succeeded
In showing them they were not needed;
And even then she had to Pay
To get the Men to go Away!

It happened that a few Weeks later
Her Aunt was off to the Theatre
To see that Interesting Play
The Second Mrs. Tanqueray.
She had refused to take her Niece
To hear this Entertaining Piece:
(A Deprivation Just and Wise
To punish her for Telling Lies.)

That night a Fire *did* break out—
You should have heard Matilda Shout!
You should have heard her Scream and Bawl,
And throw the window up and call
To People passing in the Street—
(The rapidly increasing Heat
Encouraging her to obtain
Their confidence)—but all In Vain!

For every time She shouted, "Fire!"
They only answered, "Little Liar!"
And therefore when her Aunt returned,
Matilda, and the House, were Burned.

6. **Scintillate, Scintillate, Globule Vivific** by Dave Arns

Scintillate, scintillate, globule vivific!
In vain do I ponder thy nature specific—
    Precariously poised in the ether capacious,
    Closely resembling a gem carbonaceous;
Scintillate, scintillate, globule vivific,
In vain do I ponder thy nature specific!

Level Three

7. **What I Live For** [Author Unknown]

I live for those who love me,
Whose hearts are kind and true;
For the heaven that smiles above me,
And awaits my spirit, too;
For all human ties that bind me,
For the task my God assigned me,
For the bright hopes left behind me,
And the good that I can do.

I live to learn their story,
Who suffered for my sake;
To emulate their glory,
And follow in their wake;
Bards, patriots, martyrs, sages,
The noble of all ages,
Whose deeds crown History's pages,
And Time's great volume make.

I live to hail that season,
By gifted minds foretold,
When man shall live by reason,
And not alone by gold;
When man to man united,
And every wrong thing righted,
The whole world shall be lighted
As Eden was of old.

8. **Courage** by Sister M. Eulalia, RSM

Courage is a fabric
    So woven of the soul
It shrinks with fear, stretches
    When straining toward a Goal.
But when in eyes it glows
    Awaiting tyrant's rod,
It is of mystic birth,
    Holding a tryst with God.

Level Three

9. **Grandfather's Clock** by Henry Clay Work

My grandfather's clock was too large for the shelf,
    So it stood ninety years on the floor;
It was taller by half than the old man himself,
Though it weighed not a pennyweight more.
It was bought on the morn of the day that he was born
    And was always his treasure and pride,
But it stopped short—never to go again—
    When the old man died.

    Ninety years without slumbering—
    Tick, tick, tick, tick.
    His life seconds numbering—
    Tick, tick, tick, tick.
    It stopped short—never to go again—
    When the old man died.

In watching its pendulum swing to and fro
    Many hours had he spent while a boy;
And in childhood and manhood the clock seemed to know
    And to share both his grief and his joy,
For it struck twenty-four when he entered the door
    With a blooming and beautiful bride,
But it stopped short—never to go again—
    When the old man died.

My grandfather said of those he could hire,
    Not a servant so faithful he found,
For it wasted no time and had but one desire—
    At the close of each week to be wound.
And it kept in its place—not a frown upon its face,
    And its hands never hung by its side;
But it stopped short—never to go again—
    When the old man died.

It rang an alarm in the dead of night—
    An alarm that for years had been dumb.
And we knew that his spirit was pluming for flight,
    That his hour for departure had come.
Still the clock kept the time with a soft and muffled chime
    As we silently stood by his side;
But it stopped short—never to go again—
    When the old man died.

Level Three

10. **The Touch of the Master's Hand** by Myra Brooks Welch

'Twas battered and scarred, and the auctioneer
Thought it scarcely worth his while
To waste much time on the old violin,
But held it up with a smile:
"What am I bidden, good folks," he cried,
"Who'll start the bidding for me?"
"A dollar, a dollar"; then "Two! Only two?
Two dollars, and who'll make it three?
Three dollars, once; three dollars, twice;
Going for three"—But no,
From the room, far back, a gray-haired man
Came forward and picked up the bow;
Then, wiping the dust from the old violin,
And tightening the loose strings,
He played a melody pure and sweet
As a caroling angel sings.

The music ceased, and the auctioneer,
With a voice that was quiet and low,
Said: "What am I bid for the old violin?"
And he held it up with the bow.
"A thousand dollars, and who'll make it two?
Two thousand! And who'll make it three?
Three thousand, once, three thousand, twice,
And going, and gone," said he.
The people cheered, but some of them cried,
"We do not quite understand
What changed its worth." Swift came the reply:
"The touch of a master's hand."

And many a man with life out of tune,
And battered and scarred with sin,
Is auctioned cheap to the thoughtless crowd,
Much like the old violin.
A "mess of pottage," a glass of wine;
A game—and he travels on.
He is "going" once, and "going" twice,
He's "going" and almost "gone".
But the Master comes, and the foolish crowd
Never can quite understand
The worth of a soul and the change that's wrought
By the touch of the Master's hand.

Level Three

11. **The Unknown Soldier** by Billy Rose

There's a graveyard near the White House
    Where the Unknown Soldier lies,
And the flowers there are sprinkled
    With the tears from mother's eyes.

I stood there not so long ago
    With roses for the brave,
And suddenly I heard a voice
    Speak from out the grave:

"I am the Unknown Soldier,"
    The spirit voice began,
"And I think I have the right
    To ask some questions man to man.

Are my buddies taken care of?
    Was their victory so sweet?
Is that big reward you offered
    Selling pencils on the street?

Did they really win the freedom
    They battled to achieve?
Do you still respect that Croix de Guerre
    Above that empty sleeve?

Does a gold star in the window
    Now mean anything at all?
I wonder how my old girl feels
    When she hears a bugle call.

And that baby who sang
    'Hello, Central, give me no man's land'–
Can they replace her daddy
    With a military band?

I wonder if the profiteers
    Have satisfied their greed?
I wonder if a soldier's mother
    Ever is in need?

I wonder if the kings, who planned it all
    Are really satisfied?
They played their game of checkers
    And eleven million died.

I am the Unknown Soldier
    And maybe I died in vain,
But if I were alive and my country called,
    I'd do it all over again."

Level Three

12. **The Pessimist** by Ben King & **The Optimist** [Author Unkown]

Nothing to do but work,
Nothing to eat but food;
Nothing to wear but clothes
To keep one from going nude.

Nothing to breathe but air,
Quick as a flash 'tis gone;
Nowhere to fall but off,
Nowhere to stand but on.

Nothing to comb but hair,
Nowhere to sleep but in bed;
Nothing to weep but tears,
Nothing to bury but dead.

Nothing to sing but songs;
Ah, well, alas! alack!
Nowhere to go but out,
Nowhere to come but back.

Nothing to see but sights,
Nothing to quench but thirst;
Nothing to have but what we've got;
Thus thro' life we are cursed.

Nothing to strike but a gait;
Everything moves that goes.
Nothing at all but common sense
Can ever withstand these woes.

The optimist fell ten stories,
At each window bar
He shouted to his friends,
    "All right so far."

LEVEL THREE

13. **The Fool's Prayer** by Edward Rowland Sill

The royal feast was done; the King
Sought some new sport to banish care,
And to his jester cried: "Sir Fool,
Kneel now, and make for us a prayer!"

The jester doffed his cap and bells,
And stood the mocking court before;
They could not see the bitter smile
Behind the painted grin he wore.

He bowed his head, and bent his knee
Upon the Monarch's silken stool;
His pleading voice arose: "O Lord,
Be merciful to me, a fool!

"No pity, Lord, could change the heart
From red with wrong to white as wool;
The rod must heal the sin: but Lord,
Be merciful to me, a fool!

"'Tis not by guilt the onward sweep
Of truth and right, O Lord, we stay;
'Tis by our follies that so long
We hold the earth from heaven away.

"These clumsy feet, still in the mire,
Go crushing blossoms without end;
These hard, well-meaning hands we thrust
Among the heart-strings of a friend.

"The ill-timed truth we might have kept—
Who knows how sharp it pierced and stung?
The word we had not sense to say—
Who knows how grandly it had rung!

"Our faults no tenderness should ask.
The chastening stripes must cleanse them all;
But for our blunders—oh, in shame
Before the eyes of heaven we fall.

"Earth bears no balsam for mistakes;
Men crown the knave, and scourge the tool
That did his will; but Thou, O Lord,
Be merciful to me, a fool!"

The room was hushed; in silence rose
The King, and sought his gardens cool,
And walked apart, and murmured low,
"Be merciful to me, a fool!"

14. **Casey at the Bat** by Ernest Lawrence Thayer

The outlook wasn't brilliant for the Mudville nine that day;
The score stood four to two but one inning more to play.
And then when Cooney died at first and Barrows did the same,
A sickly silence fell upon the patrons of the game.

A straggling few got up to go in deep despair. The rest
Clung to the hope which springs eternal in the human breast;
They thought if only Casey could but get a whack at that—
We'd put up even money now with Casey at the bat.

But Flynn preceded Casey, as did also Jimmy Blake,
And the former was a lulu and the latter was a cake;
So upon that stricken multitude grim melancholy sat,
For there seemed but little chance of Casey's getting to the bat.

But Flynn let drive a single, to the wonderment of all,
And Blake, the much despised, tore the cover off the ball;
And when the dust had lifted, and the men saw what had occurred,
There was Jimmy safe at second and Flynn a-hugging third.

(Continued on next page)

(Casey at the Bat, continued)

Then from five thousand throats and more there rose a lusty yell;
It rumbled through the valley, it rattled in the dell;
It knocked upon the mountain and recoiled upon the flat,
For Casey, mighty Casey, was advancing to the bat.

There was ease in Casey's manner as he stepped into his place;
There was pride in Casey's bearing and a smile on Casey's face.
And when, responding to the cheers, he lightly doffed his hat,
No stranger in the crowd could doubt 'twas Casey at the bat.

Ten thousand eyes were on him as he rubbed his hands with dirt;
Five thousand tongues applauded when he wiped them on his shirt.
Then while the writhing pitcher ground the ball into his hip,
Defiance gleamed in Casey's eye, a sneer curled Casey's lip.

And now the leather-covered sphere came hurtling through the air,
And Casey stood a-watching it in haughty grandeur there.
Close by the sturdy batsman the ball unheeded sped—
"That ain't my style," said Casey. "Strike one," the umpire said.

From the benches, black with people, there went up a muffled roar,
Like the beating of the storm waves on a stern and distant shore.
"Kill him! Kill the umpire!" shouted someone on the stand;
And it's likely they'd have killed him had not Casey raised his hand.

With a smile of Christian charity great Casey's visage shone;
He stilled the rising tumult; he bade the game go on;
He signaled to the pitcher, and once more the spheroid flew;
But Casey still ignored it, and the umpire said, "Strike two."

"Fraud!" cried the maddened thousands, and echo answered, "Fraud!"
But one scornful look from Casey and the audience was awed.
They saw his face grow stern and cold, they saw his muscles strain,
And they knew that Casey wouldn't let that ball go by again.

The sneer is gone from Casey's lip, his teeth are clenched in hate;
He pounds with cruel violence his bat upon the plate.
And now the pitcher holds the ball, and now he lets it go,
And now the air is shattered by the force of Casey's blow.

Oh, somewhere in this favored land the sun is shining bright;
The band is playing somewhere, and somewhere hearts are light,
And somewhere men are laughing, and somewhere children shout;
But there is no joy in Mudville—mighty Casey has struck out.

Level Three

15. **He Wishes for the Cloths of Heaven** by W.B. Yeats

Had I the heavens' embroidered cloths,
Enwrought with golden and silver light,
The blue and the dim and the dark cloths
Of night and light and the half-light,
I would spread the cloths under your feet;
But I, being poor, have only my dreams;
I have spread my dreams under your feet;
Tread softly because you tread on my dreams.

16. **The Destruction of Sennacherib** by Lord Byron

The Assyrian came down like the wolf on the fold,
And his cohorts were gleaming in purple and gold;
And the sheen of their spears was like stars on the sea,
When the blue wave rolls nightly on deep Galilee.

Like the leaves of the forest when Summer is green,
That host with their banners at sunset were seen:
Like the leaves of the forest when Autumn hath flown,
That host on the morrow lay withered and strown.

For the Angel of Death spread his wings on the blast,
And breathed in the face of the foe as he passed;
And the eyes of the sleepers waxed deadly and chill,
And their hearts but once heaved, and forever grew still.

And there lay the steed with his nostril all wide,
But through it there rolled not the breath of his pride;
And the foam of his gasping lay white on the turf,
And cold as the spray of the rock-beating surf.

And there lay the rider distorted and pale,
With the dew on his brow, and the rust on his mail;
And the tents were all silent, the banners alone,
The lances unlifted, the trumpet unblown.

And the widows of Ashur are loud in their wail,
And the idols are broke in the temple of Baal;
And the might of the Gentile, unsmote by the sword,
Hath melted like snow in the glance of the Lord!

Level Three

17. **The Village Blacksmith** by Henry Wadsworth Longfellow

Under a spreading chestnut-tree
The village smithy stands;
The smith, a mighty man is he,
With large and sinewy hands;
And the muscles of his brawny arms
Are strong as iron bands.

His hair is crisp, and black, and long,
His face is like the tan;
His brow is wet with honest sweat,
He earns whate'er he can,
And looks the whole world
    in the face,
For he owes not any man.

Week in, week out,
    from morn till night,
You can hear his bellows blow;
You can hear him
    swing his heavy sledge,
With measured beat and slow,
Like a sexton ringing the village bell,
When the evening sun is low.

And children coming
    home from school
Look in at the open door;
They love to see the flaming forge,
And hear the bellows roar,
And catch the burning sparks that fly
Like chaff from a threshing-floor.

He goes on Sunday to the church,
And sits among his boys;
He hears the parson pray and preach,
He hears his daughter's voice,
Singing in the village choir,
And it makes his heart rejoice.

It sounds to him like her mother's voice,
Singing in Paradise!
He needs must think of her once more,
How in the grave she lies;
And with his hard, rough hand he wipes
A tear out of his eyes.

Toiling,—rejoicing,—sorrowing,
Onward through life he goes;
Each morning sees some task begin,
Each evening sees it close;
Something attempted, something done,
Has earned a night's repose.

Thanks, thanks to thee, my worthy friend,
For the lesson thou hast taught!
Thus at the flaming forge of life
Our fortunes must be wrought;
Thus on its sounding anvil shaped
Each burning deed and thought

Level Three

18. **When I Heard the Learn'd Astronomer** by Walt Whitman

WHEN I heard the learn'd astronomer;
When the proofs, the figures, were ranged in columns before me;
When I was shown the charts and the diagrams,
    to add, divide, and measure them;
When I, sitting, heard the astronomer,
    where he lectured with much applause in the lecture-room,
How soon, unaccountable, I became tired and sick;
Till rising and gliding out, I wander'd off by myself,
In the mystical moist night-air, and from time to time,
Look'd up in perfect silence at the stars.

19. **Casey's Revenge** by Grantland Rice

There were saddened hearts in Mudville for a week or even more;
There were muttered oaths and curses—every fan in town was sore.
"Just think," said one, "how soft it looked with Casey at the bat!
And then to think he'd go and spring a bush-league trick like that."

All his past fame was forgotten; he was now a hopeless "shine",
They called him "Strike-out Casey" from the mayor down the line,
And as he came to bat each day his bosom heaved a sigh,
While a look of helpless fury shone in mighty Casey's eye.

The lane is long, someone has said, that never turns again,
And fate, though fickle, often gives another chance to men.
And Casey smiled—his rugged face no longer wore a frown;
The pitcher who had started all the trouble came to town.

All Mudville had assembled; ten thousand fans had come
To see the twirler who had put big Casey on the bum;
And when he stepped into the box the multitude went wild.
He doffed his cap in proud disdain—but Casey only smiled.

"Play ball!" the umpire's voice rang out, and then the game began;
But in that throng of thousands there was not a single fan
Who thought that Mudville had a chance; and with the setting sun
Their hopes sank low—the rival team was leading "four to one".

(Continued on next page)

LEVEL THREE

(Casey's Revenge, continued)

The last half of the ninth came round, with no change in the score;
But when the first man up hit safe the crowd began to roar.
The din increased, the echo of ten thousand shouts was heard
When the pitcher hit the second and gave "four balls" to the third.

Three men on base—nobody out—three runs to tie the game!
A triple meant the highest niche in Mudville's hall of fame;
But here the rally ended and the gloom was deep as night
When the fourth one "fouled to catcher" and the fifth "flew out to right".

A dismal groan in chorus came—a scowl was on each face—
When Casey walked up, bat in hand, and slowly took his place;
His bloodshot eyes in fury gleamed; his teeth were clinched in hate;
He gave his cap a vicious hook and pounded on the plate.

But fame is fleeting as the wind, and glory fades away;
There were no wild and wooly cheers, no glad acclaim this day.
They hissed and groaned and hooted as they clamored, "Strike him out!"
But Casey gave no outward sign that he had heard this shout.

The pitcher smiled and cut one loose; across the plate it spread;
Another hiss, another groan. "Strike one!" the umpire said.
Zip! Like a shot, the second curve broke just below his knee—
"Strike two!" the umpire roared aloud; but Casey made no plea.

No roasting for the umpire now—his was an easy lot;
But here the pitcher whirled again—was that a rifle shot?
A whack! a crack! and out through space the leather pellet flew,
A blot against the distant sky, a speck against the blue.

Above the fence in center field, in rapid whirling flight,
The sphere sailed on; the blot grew dim and then was lost to sight.
Ten thousand hats were thrown in air, ten thousand threw a fit;
But no one ever found the ball that mighty Casey hit.

Oh, somewhere in this favored land dark clouds may hide the sun,
And somewhere bands no longer play and children have no fun;
And somewhere over blighted lives there hangs a heavy pall;
But Mudville hearts are happy now—for Casey hit the ball!

20. Personal Selection (any length)

Level Three

Level Four

Level Four Poems

1. **The Embarrassing Episode of Little Miss Muffet** by Guy Wetmore Carryl — 62
2. **The Tiger** by William Blake — 63
3. **Metaphysics** by Oliver Herford — 63
4. **Lochinvar** by Sir Walter Scott — 64
5. **The Choir Invisible** by George Eliot — 65
6. **The Hand That Rocks The Cradle . . .** by W.R. Wallace — 66
7. **The Maldive Shark** by Herman Melville — 66
8. **The Quality of Mercy** from *The Merchant of Venice* by William Shakespeare — 67
9. **In Flanders Fields** by Dr. John McCrae — 67
10. **Epigram** by Samuel Coleridge — 68
11. **God Save the Flag** by Oliver Wendell Holmes — 68
12. **The Sycophantic Fox and the Gullible Raven** by Guy Wetmore Carryl — 69
13. **A Song from the Suds** by Louisa May Alcott — 70
14. **The Hen** by Oliver Herford — 70
15. **Desiderata** by Max Ehrmann — 71
16. **Woodman, Spare that Tree** George Perkins Morris — 72
17. **Grand Chorus** by John Dryden — 73
18. **An Overworked Elocutionist** by Carolyn Wells — 73
19. **The Hunting of the Dragon** by Gilbert Keith Chesterton — 74
20. Personal Selection (any length) — 74

NOTES:

If, by chance, the student has never heard the short nursery rhyme of "Little Miss Muffet," they should become familiar with it before memorizing Carryl's version.

Narrative poems like "Lochinvar" can be studied and rewritten according to the Story Sequence Chart, which is part of the IEW Structure & Style syllabus. Such rewriting will greatly enhance understanding of the poem itself.

There are many web links to McCrae's poem "In Flanders Fields," which would well accompany a study of World War I.

"The Hen" is obviously a satire of Kilmer's "Trees" (memorized in Level Two) with numerous other humorous and social allusions. A careful study of the poem will bring much mirth.

In "An Overworked Elocutionist" the student will find bits of several poems already learned, as well as lines from several famous works not included in this anthology. Finding and reading the originals will certainly add to the enjoyment of knowing this one.

Level Four

1. **The Embarrassing Episode of Little Miss Muffet** by Guy Wetmore Carryl

Little Miss Muffet discovered a tuffet,
    (Which never occurred to the rest of us)
and, as 'twas a June day, and just about noonday,
    She wanted to eat—like the best of us:
Her diet was whey, and I hasten to say
    It is wholesome and people grow fat on it.
The spot being lonely, the lady not only
    Discovered the tuffet, but sat on it.

A rivulet gabbled beside her and babbled,
    As rivulets always are thought to do,
And dragonflies sported around and cavorted,
    As poets say dragonflies ought to do;
When, glancing aside for a moment, she spied
    A horrible sight that brought fear to her,
A hideous spider was sitting beside her,
    And most unavoidably near to her!

Albeit unsightly, this creature politely
    Said: "Madam, I earnestly vow to you,
I'm penitent that I did not bring my hat. I
    Should otherwise certainly bow to you."
Though anxious to please, he was so ill at ease
    That he lost all his sense of propriety,
And grew so inept that he clumsily stept
    In her plate—which is barred in Society.

This curious error completed her terror;
    She shuddered, and growing much paler, not
Only left tuffet, but dealt him a buffet
    Which doubled him up in a sailor knot.
It should be explained that at this he was pained:
    He cried: "I have vexed you, no doubt of it!
Your fist's like a truncheon." "You're still in my luncheon,"
    Was all that she answered. "Get out of it!"

And the *Moral* is this: Be it madam or miss
    To whom you have something to say,
You are only absurd when you get in the curd
    But you're rude when you get in the whey!

Level Four

2. **The Tiger** by William Blake

Tiger, tiger, burning bright,
In the forests of the night,
What immortal hand or eye
Could frame thy fearful symmetry?

In what distant deeps or skies
Burnt the fire of thine eyes?
On what wings dare he aspire?
What the hand dare seize the fire?

And what shoulder, and what art,
Could twist the sinews of thy heart?
And when thy heart began to beat,
What dread hand and what dread feet?

What the hammer? What the chain?
In what furnace was thy brain?
What the anvil? What dread grasp
Dare its deadly terrors clasp?

When the stars threw down their spears,
And water'd heaven with their tears,
Did He smile His work to see?
Did He who made the Lamb, make thee?

Tiger, tiger, burning bright,
In the forests of the night,
What immortal hand or eye
Dare frame thy fearful symmetry?

3. **Metaphysics** by Oliver Herford

Why and Wherefore set out one day
To hunt for a wild Negation.
They agreed to meet at a cool retreat
On the Point of Interrogation.

But the night was dark and they missed their mark,
And, driven well-nigh to distraction,
They lost their ways in a murky maze
Of utter abstruse abstraction.

Then they took a boat and were soon afloat
On a Sea of Speculation,
But the sea grew rough, and their boat, though tough,
Was split into an Equation.

As they floundered about in the Waves of Doubt
Rose a fearful Hypothesis,
Who gibbered with glee as they sank in the sea,
And the last they saw was this:

On a rock-bound Reef of Unbelief
There sat the wild Negation;
Then they sank once more and were washed ashore
At the Point of Interrogation.

Level Four

4. **Lochinvar** by Sir Walter Scott

O, young Lochinvar is come out of the west,
Through all the wide Border his steed was the best,
And save his good broadsword he weapons had none;
He rode all unarmed, and he rode all alone.
So faithful in love, and so dauntless in war,
There never was knight like the young Lochinvar.

He stayed not for brake, and he stopped not for stone,
He swam the Eske river where ford there was none;
But, ere he alighted at Netherby gate,
The bride had consented, the gallant came late:
For a laggard in love, and a dastard in war,
Was to wed the fair Ellen of brave Lochinvar.

So boldly he entered the Netherby hall,
Among bride's-men and kinsmen, and brothers and all;
Then spoke the bride's father, his hand on his sword
(For the poor craven bridegroom said never a word),
"O come ye in peace here, or come ye in war,
Or to dance at our bridal, young Lord Lochinvar?"

"I long wooed your daughter, my suit you denied;—
Love swells like the Solway, but ebbs like its tide—
And now I am come, with this lost love of mine,
To lead but one measure, drink one cup of wine.
There are maidens in Scotland more lovely by far,
That would gladly be bride to the young Lochinvar."

The bride kissed the goblet; the knight took it up,
He quaffed off the wine, and he threw down the cup,
She looked down to blush, and she looked up to sigh,
With a smile on her lips and a tear in her eye.
He took her soft hand, ere her mother could bar,—
"Now tread we a measure!" said young Lochinvar.

So stately his form, and so lovely her face,
That never a hall such a galliard did grace;
While her mother did fret, and her father did fume,
And the bridegroom stood dangling his bonnet and plume;
And the bride-maidens whispered, "'Twere better by far
To have matched our fair cousin with young Lochinvar."

Continued on next page

Lochinvar, continued

One touch to her hand, and one word in her ear,
When they reached the hall door, and the charger stood near;
So light to the croupe the fair lady he swung,
So light to the saddle before her he sprung!
"She is won! We are gone, over bank, bush, and scaur;
They'll have fleet steeds that follow," quoth young Lochinvar.

There was mounting 'mong Graemes of the Netherby clan;
Forsters, Fenwicks, and Musgraves, they rode and they ran;
There was racing, and chasing, on Cannobie Lee,
But the lost bride of Netherby ne'er did they see.
So daring in love, and so dauntless in war,
Have ye e'er heard of gallant like young Lochinvar?

5. **The Choir Invisible** by George Eliot

O, may I join the choir invisible
Of those immortal dead who live again
In minds made better by their presence; live
In pulses stirred to generosity,
In deeds of daring rectitude, in scorn
Of miserable aims that end with self,
In thoughts sublime that pierce the night like stars,
And with their mild persistence urge men's minds
To vaster issues....

May I reach
That purest heaven—be to other souls
The cup of strength in some great agony,
Enkindle generous ardor, feed pure love,
Beget the smiles that have no cruelty,
Be the sweet presence of good diffused,
And in diffusion ever more intense!
So shall I join the choir invisible,
Whose music is the gladness of the world.

Level Four

6. **The Hand That Rocks The Cradle Is The Hand That Rules The World**
   by William Ross Wallace

Blessings on the hand of woman!
Angels guard its strength and grace,
In the palace, cottage, hovel,
Oh, no matter where the place;
Would that never storms assailed it,
Rainbows ever gently curled;
For the hand that rocks the cradle
Is the hand that rules the world.

Infancy's the tender fountain,
Power may with beauty flow,
Mother's first to guide the streamlets,
From them souls unresting grow—
Grow on for the good or evil,
Sunshine streamed or evil hurled;
For the hand that rocks the cradle
Is the hand that rules the world.

Woman, how divine your mission
Here upon our natal sod!
Keep, oh, keep the young heart open
Always to the breath of God!
All true trophies of the ages
Are from mother-love impearled;
For the hand that rocks the cradle
Is the hand that rules the world.

Blessings on the hand of women!
Fathers, sons, and daughters cry,
And the sacred song is mingled
With the worship in the sky—
Mingles where no tempest darkens,
Rainbows evermore are hurled;
For the hand that rocks the cradle
Is the hand that rules the world.

7. **The Maldive Shark** by Herman Melville

About the Shark, phlegmatical one,
Pale sot of the Maldive sea,
The sleek little pilot-fish, azure and slim,
How alert in attendance be.
From his saw-pit of mouth, from his charnel of maw,
They have nothing of harm to dread,
But liquidly glide on his ghastly flank
Or before his Gorgonian head;
Or lurk in the port of serrated teeth
In white triple tiers of glittering gates,
And there find a haven when peril's abroad,
An asylum in jaws of the Fates!
They are friends; and friendly they guide him to prey,
Yet never partake of the treat—
Eyes and brains to the dotard lethargic and dull,
Pale ravener of horrible meat.

LEVEL FOUR

8. **The Quality of Mercy** from *The Merchant of Venice* by William Shakespeare

The quality of mercy is not strain'd.
It droppeth as the gentle rain from heaven
Upon the place beneath. It is twice blest:
It blesseth him that gives, and him that takes.
'Tis mightiest in the mightiest; it becomes
The thronèd monarch better than his crown.
His scepter shows the force of temporal power,
The attribute to awe and majesty,
Wherein doth sit the dread and fear of kings;
But mercy is above this sceptered sway;
It is enthroned in the hearts of kings;
It is an attribute to God himself;
And earthly power doth then show likest God's
When mercy seasons justice.

9. **In Flanders Fields** by Dr. John McCrae

In Flanders fields the poppies blow
Between the crosses, row on row,
That marked our place; and in the sky
The larks, still bravely singing, fly
Scarce heard amid the guns below.

We are the dead. Short days ago
We lived, felt dawn, saw sunset glow,
Loved and were loved, and now we lie
    In Flanders fields.

Take up our quarrel with the foe:
To you from failing hands we throw the torch;
Be yours to hold it high.
If ye break faith with us who die
We shall not sleep, though poppies grow
    In Flanders fields.

Level Four

10. **Epigram** by Samuel Coleridge

Sir, I admit your general rule,
That every poet is a fool,
But you yourself may serve to show it,
That every fool is not a poet.

11. **God Save the Flag** by Oliver Wendell Holmes

Washed in the blood of the brave and the blooming,
Snatched from the altars of insolent foes,
Burning with star-fires, but never consuming,
Flash its broad ribbons of lily and rose.

Vainly the prophets of Baal would rend it,
Vainly his worshippers pray for its fall;
Thousands have died for it, millions defend it,
Emblem of justice and mercy to all;

Justice that reddens the sky with her terrors,
Mercy that comes with her white-handed train,
Soothing all passions, redeeming all errors,
Sheathing the sabre and breaking the chain.

Borne on the deluge of all usurpations,
Drifted our Ark o'er the desolate seas,
Bearing the rainbow of hope to the nations,
Torn from the storm-cloud and flung to the breeze!

God bless the Flag and its loyal defenders,
While its broad folds o'er the battle-field wave,
Till the dim star-wreath rekindle its splendors,
Washed from its stains in the blood of the brave!

Level Four

12. **The Sycophantic Fox and the Gullible Raven** by Guy Wetmore Carryl

A raven sat upon a tree,
    And not a word he spoke, for
His beak contained a piece of Brie,
    Or, maybe, it was Roquefort:
    We'll make it any kind you please—
At all events, it was a cheese.

Beneath the tree's umbrageous limb
    A hungry fox sat smiling;
He saw the raven watching him,
    And spoke in words beguiling:
    "*J'admire*," said he, "*ton plumage*,"
(The which was simply persiflage).

Two things there are, no doubt you know,
    To which a fox is used,—
A rooster that is bound to crow,
    A crow that's bound to roost,
    And whichsoever he espies
He tells the most unblushing lies.

"Sweet fowl," he said, "I understand
    You're more than merely natty:
I hear you sing to beat the band
    And Adelina Patti.
    Pray render with your liquid tongue
    A bit from 'Götterdämmerung!'"

This subtle speech was aimed to please
    The crow, and it succeeded;
He thought no bird in all the trees
    Could sing as well as he did.
    In flattery completely doused,
He gave the "Jewel Song" from "Faust."

But gravitation's law, of course,
    As Isaac Newton showed it,
Exerted on the cheese its force,
    And elsewhere soon bestowed it.
    In fact, there is no need to tell
What happened when to earth it fell.

I blush to add that when the bird
    Took in the situation,
He said one brief, emphatic word,
    Unfit for publication.
    The fox was greatly startled, but
He only sighed and answered "Tut!"

The moral is: A fox is bound
    To be a shameless sinner.
And also: When the cheese comes round
    You know it's after dinner.
    But (what is only known to few)
    The fox is after dinner, too.

Level Four

13. **A Song from the Suds** by Louisa May Alcott

Queen of my tub, I merrily sing,
While the white foam raises high,
And sturdily wash, and rinse, and wring,
And fasten the clothes to dry;
Then out in the free fresh air they swing,
Under the sunny sky.

I wish we could wash from our hearts and our souls
The stains of the week away,
And let water and air by their magic make
Ourselves as pure as they;
Then on the earth there would be indeed
A glorious washing day!

Along the path of a useful life
Will heart's-ease ever bloom;
The busy mind has no time to think
Of sorrow, or care, or gloom;
And anxious thoughts may be swept away
As we busily wield a broom.

I am glad a task to me is given
To labor at day by day;
For it brings me health, and strength, and hope,
And I cheerfully learn to say—
"Head, you may think; heart, you may feel;
But hand, you shall work always!"

14. **The Hen** by Oliver Herford

Alas, my Child, where is the Pen
That can do Justice to the Hen?
Like Royalty, She goes her way,
Laying foundations every day,
Though not for Public Buildings, yet
For Custard, Cake and Omelette.
Or if too Old for such a use
They have their Fling at some Abuse,
As when to Censure Plays Unfit
Upon the Stage they make a Hit,
Or at elections Seal the Fate
Of an Obnoxious Candidate.
No wonder, Child, we prize the Hen,
Whose Egg is mightier than the Pen.

Level Four

15. **Desiderata** by Max Ehrmann

Go placidly amid the noise and the haste,
    and remember what peace there may be in silence.
As far as possible, without surrender,
    be on good terms with all persons.
Speak your truth quietly and clearly,
    and listen to others, even to the dull and the ignorant; they too have their story.
Avoid loud and aggressive persons; they are vexatious to the spirit.

If you compare yourself with others, you may become vain or bitter,
    for always there will be greater and lesser persons than yourself.
Enjoy your achievements as well as your plans.
Keep interested in your own career, however humble;
    it is a real possession in the changing fortunes of time.

Exercise caution in your business affairs, for the world is full of trickery.
But let this not blind you to what virtue there is;
    many persons strive for high ideals, and everywhere life is full of heroism.
Be yourself. Especially do not feign affection.
Neither be cynical about love, for in the face of all aridity and disenchantment,
    it is as perennial as the grass.

Take kindly the counsel of the years, gracefully surrendering the things of youth.
Nurture strength of spirit to shield you in sudden misfortune.
But do not distress yourself with dark imaginings.
Many fears are born of fatigue and loneliness.

Beyond a wholesome discipline, be gentle with yourself.
You are a child of the universe no less than the trees and the stars;
    you have a right to be here.
And whether or not it is clear to you,
    no doubt the universe is unfolding as it should.

Therefore be at peace with God, whatever you conceive Him to be.
And whatever your labors and aspirations,
    in the noisy confusion of life, keep peace in your soul.
With all its sham, drudgery, and broken dreams, it is still a beautiful world.
Be cheerful.
Strive to be happy.

16. **Woodman, Spare that Tree** by George Perkins Morris

Woodman, spare that tree!
    Touch not a single bough!
In youth it sheltered me,
    And I'll protect it now.
'Twas my forefather's hand
    That placed it near his cot;
There, woodman, let it stand,
    Thy axe shall harm it not!

That old familiar tree,
    Whose glory and renown
Are spread o'er land and sea,
    And wouldst thou hew it down?
Woodman, forbear thy stroke!
    Cut not its earth-bound ties;
O, spare that aged oak,
    Now towering to the skies!

When but an idle boy
    I sought its grateful shade;
In all their gushing joy
    Here too my sisters played.
My mother kissed me here;
    My father pressed my hand—
Forgive this foolish tear,
    But let that old oak stand!

My heart-strings round thee cling,
    Close as thy bark, old friend!
Here shall the wild-bird sing,
    And still thy branches bend.
Old tree! The storm still brave!
    And woodman, leave the spot;
While I've a hand to save,
    Thy axe shall hurt it not.

Level Four

17. **Grand Chorus** by John Dryden

As from the power of sacred lays
The spheres begin to move,
And sung to the Creator's praise
To all the blessed above;
So when the last and dreadful hour
This crumbling pageant shall devour,
The trumpet shall be heard on high,
The dead shall live, the living die,
And music shall untune the sky.

18. **An Overworked Elocutionist** by Carolyn Wells

Once there was a little boy whose name was Robert Reese;
And every Friday afternoon he had to speak a piece.
So many poems thus he learned, that soon he had a store
Of recitations in his head and still kept learning more.

And now this is what happened: He was called upon one week
And totally forgot the piece he was about to speak.
His brain he cudgeled. Not a word remained within his head!
And so he spoke at random, and this is what he said:

"My beautiful, my beautiful, who standest proudly by,
It was the schooner Hesperus—the breaking waves dashed high!
Why is this Forum crowded? What means this stir in Rome!
Under a spreading chestnut tree, there is no place like home!

When freedom from her mountain height cried, 'Twinkle, little star,'
Shoot if you must this old gray head, King Henry of Navarre!
Roll on, thou deep and dark blue castled crag of Drachenfels,
My name is Norval, on the Grampian Hills, ring out, wild bells!

If you're waking, call me early. To be or not to be,
The curfew must not ring tonight! Oh, woodman, spare that tree!
Charge, Chester, charge! On, Stanley, on! And let who will be clever!
The boy stood on the burning deck, but I go on forever!"

His elocution was superb, his voice and gestures fine;
His schoolmates all applauded as he finished the last line.
"I see it doesn't matter," Robert thought, "what words I say,
So long as I declaim with oratorical display."

Level Four

19. **The Hunting of the Dragon** by G. K. Chesterton

When we went hunting the Dragon
In the days when we were young,
We tossed the bright world
      over our shoulder
As bugle and baldrick slung;
Never was world so wild and fair
As what went by on the wind,

Never such fields of paradise
As the fields we left behind;
For this is the best of a rest for men
That men should rise and ride
Making a flying fairyland
Of market and country-side,
Wings on the cottage,
      wings on the wood,
Wings upon pot and pan,
For the hunting of the Dragon
That is the life of a man.

For men grow weary of fairyland
When the Dragon is a dream,
And tire of the talking bird in the tree,
The singing fish in the stream;
And the wandering stars grow stale,
      grow stale,
And the wonder is stiff with scorn;
For this is the honour of fairyland
And the following of the horn;

Beauty on beauty called us back
When we could rise and ride,
And a woman looked
      out of every window
As wonderful as a bride;
And the tavern-sign as a tabard blazed,
And the children cheered and ran,
For the love of the hate of the Dragon
That is the pride of a man.

The sages called him a shadow
And the light went out of the sun;
And the wise men told us
      that all was well
And all was weary and one;
And then, and then, in the quiet garden,
With never a weed to kill,
We knew that his shining tail had shone
In the white road over the hill;
We knew that the clouds were flakes of flame,
We knew that the sunset fire
Was red with the blood of the Dragon
Whose death is the world's desire.

For the horn was blown
      in the heart of the night
That men should rise and ride,
Keeping the tryst of a terrible jest
Never for long untried;
Drinking a dreadful blood for wine,
Never in cup or can,
The death of a deathless Dragon,
That is the life of a man.

20. Personal Selection (any length)

LEVEL FIVE: SPEECH & SOLILOQUY SUGGESTIONS

- St. Francis's Sermon to the Birds
- Excerpt from Patrick Henry's speech to Virginia Delegation ending with, "Give me liberty or give me death!"
- Excerpt from Women in Politics speech by Lady Astor: "…I can conceive of nothing worse than a man-governed world except a woman-governed world…"
- Excerpt from Lincoln's Nomination to the Senate: "…I believe this government cannot endure permanently half slave and half free…"
- Excerpt from 2nd Inaugural Address of Lincoln: "With malice toward none, with charity toward all…"
- Excerpt from Booker T. Washington's speech, "The American Standard" before Harvard Alumni: "…Why you have called me from the Black Belt of the South…"
- Excerpt from "The Strenuous Life," T. Roosevelt, 1899:
"The timid man, the lazy man, the man who distrusts his country, the overcivilized man…"
- Excerpt from Woodrow Wilson's "Peace Without Victory" speech before the Senate, 1917
- Excerpt in great part from Ghandi's "Non-Cooperation" speech, 1920: "…there shall be no cooperation between injustice and justice…"
- Excerpt from Churchill's "Their Finest Hour" speech
- Excerpt from Churchill's "Blood, Sweat, and Tears" address
- Excerpts from Pius XII Easter Address, 1941: "In the lamentable spectacle of human conflict which we are now witnessing…"
- Excerpt from FDR's 1st Inaugural Address: "…The only thing we have to fear is fear itself…"
- George Graham Vest: "A Tribute to the Dog"
- Excerpt from "No More War", Paul VI's 1965 address to the UN

The following recommendations may be found at the sites provided:

Excerpts from the Declaration of Independence, the Constitution, the Amendments and the Bill of Rights www.archives.gov/national_archives_experience/charters

Gettysburg Address www.ourdocuments.gov/doc.php?doc=36&page=transcript

Excerpt from FDR's 2nd Inaugural Address 1-20-37: "…Government is competent when" www.re-quest.net/history/inaugurals/fdr/second.htm

Excerpt from LBJ's Special Message to the Congress: The American Promise given March 15, 1965, in which he proposes the Voting Rights Act following Civil Rights March in Selma, Alabama: "…Our mission is at once the oldest…" www.inspiredspeeches.com/politics/lbjs-address-we-shall-overcome

Excerpt from "The Four Freedoms Speech", FDR's State of the Union Address 1-6-41: "In the future days…we look forward to a world founded upon four essential human

LEVEL FIVE: SPEECH & SOLILOQUY SUGGESTIONS

freedoms…anywhere in the world."
www.americanrhetoric.com/speeches/fdrthefourfreedoms.htm

Entire "The Great Crusade" speech, D.D. Eisenhower, June 6,1944
http://www.kansasheritage.org/abilene/ikespeech.html

From Shakespeare:

Shylock's soliloquy, *Merchant of Venice III, i* If you prick us do we not bleed…

Brutus's soliloquy, *Julius Caesar III, ii* Romans, countrymen, and lovers! Hear me for my cause…

Antony, *III, ii* "Friends, Romans, countrymen, lend me your ears…"

Rosalind's fiery soliloquy, *As You Like It III, v* "And why I pray you?…"

Jacque's oration, *As You Like It II,vii* "All the world's a stage…"

Friar Lawrence in response to Romeo's banishment behavior, *Romeo and Juliet III,iii*
"Hold thy desperate hand. Art thou a man? Thy form cries out thou art…"

Juliet before taking the sleeping potion *IV,iii* Farewell! "God knows when we shall meet again…"

Juliet on balcony *II, ii* "O Romeo, Romeo! Wherefore art thou Romeo?…"

Romeo on balcony *II, ii* "But soft, what light through yonder window breaks?…"

Romeo before his suicide, *V,iii* In faith, I will. Let me peruse this face: Mercutio's kinsman, noble Count Paris…

Amien's song, *As You Like It II,vii* "Blow, blow thou winter wind…"

Richard's opening soliloquy, *Richard III* "Now is the winter of our discontent…"

Hamlet's soliloquy, "To be or not to be…"

Macbeth *V,v* "Tomorrow, and tomorrow, and tomorrow…"

Macbeth *II, i* "Is this a dagger which I see before me?"

POET BIOGRAPHIES

Growing up in New England surrounded by her father's peers—among whom were Hawthorne, Emerson and Thoreau—the prodigious author **Louisa May Alcott** (1832-1888) wrote books, plays, poems, and short stories. Her outstanding novels wove charming tales about families like her own. Her greatest books *Little Women, Little Men,* and *Jo's Boys* are considered classics of American Literature.

Dave Arns is achieving literary notoriety with his amusing thesaurusoetry. His recent collection *Mother Goose, Ph.D* was imagineered in 1987. Thesaurusoetry challenges the reader to translate intellectual, technical verbiage into what are actually familiar rhymes that have been cleverly obscured through the use of synonyms.

Hilaire Belloc (1870-1953) was a prolific writer of novels, poetry and essays; a captivating speaker, he toured the United States. Belloc, usually embroiled in controversy, held a seat in Parliament. Along with his contemporary G.K. Chesterton, he espoused moral and economic theories that denounced Socialism and favored both small farmers and businesses.

William John Bennett was born in 1943 of a middle class family. He grew up in Brooklyn, New York and became a scholar and a teacher, stating that heroic American men such as Abraham Lincoln and Roy Campanella were his role models.

William Blake (1757-1827) was artistically gifted in writing, engraving, drawing and painting. He was born and raised in England, and he reported that his mystical writings and spiritual works of art followed from the visions he received of the angels and saints. "The Tiger" is his most famous poem.

Intriguingly reputed as a "haughty and aristocratic genius", **George Gordon, Lord Byron** (1788-1824) is one of the most important English poets. He wrote tender love ballads like "She Walks in Beauty" as well as exciting battle poems such as "The Eve of Waterloo". He died from a fever when he was only thirty-six after being caught in the rain while horseback riding.

Sir **Lewis Carroll**'s real name was Charles Dodgson. Having been homeschooled in England by his mother until the age of twelve, he wrote essays, short stories, books, and poetry from his earliest adolescence, and created such curious characters as the Mock Turtle, the Cheshire Cat and the Jabberwocky. The heroine of his phenomenally successful book *Alice's Adventures in Wonderland* seems to have been named after a favorite sister. He lived from 1832 to 1898.

Guy Wetmore Carryl (1873-1904) was an American humorist. He authored over a dozen books including novels and poetry collections. Some critics have called him flippant. The parody "The Embarrassing Episode of Little Miss Muffet" is from a larger work, *Fables for the Frivolous.*

Poet Biographies

Authors George Bernard Shaw, C.S. Lewis, and T.S Eliot were deeply influenced by **G.K. Chesterton** (1874-1936). He has been one of the greatest writers and apologists for the Christian faith in the twentieth century. He authored some one hundred books including the classics *The Everlasting Man* and *Orthodoxy,* and also wrote poetry, the Father Brown mystery series, and humor. Chesterton observed, "A good novel tells us the truth about its hero, but a bad novel tells us the truth about its author."

Another English writer, **Samuel Taylor Coleridge** (1772-1834) co-authored a volume of verse with William Wordsworth. He originated the phrases, "water, water everywhere but not a drop to drink" and "an albatross around one's neck." He is best known for his poem "The Rime of the Ancient Mariner."

Walter de la Mare (1873-1956) is remembered for his children's literature. He first began writing seriously while working as an accountant, jotting down poems during free moments. "The Listeners" is probably his most famous poem.

In this century, **John Dryden** (1631-1700) is recognized for translations of works by Virgil; he is also known for his poetry having to do with the politics of England during the Tudor monarchies and following. However while he was alive he achieved fame through his plays. "Grand Chorus" is the final verse of a larger work entitled "A Song for St. Cecilia's Day."

Paul Laurence Dunbar (1872-1906) was the son of two freed African American slaves; because they passed on their oral tradition, he was able to champion black Americans by way of his songs, fiction, and poetry. He has been called the Poet Laureate of the Negro Race, and during his lifetime Frederick Douglas, W.E.B. Du Bois, and Booker T. Washington praised his work. Other outstanding poems include "We Wear the Mask" and "Sympathy." In the latter, Dunbar penned the poignant words, "I know why the caged bird sings."

Max Ehrmann (1872-1945) became a successful lawyer, however he chose to write full time when he was forty. The prose-poem "Desiderata" first gained him literary acclaim; in addition to poetry he published books, essays, and pamphlets.

George Eliot was the pseudonym of British author Mary Ann Evans (1819-80), who wrote the novels *The Mill on the Floss* and *Silas Marner.* She used a pen name in order to guard her privacy and ensure that her work was taken seriously. Eliot is compared to Jane Austen because she attempted to expose the hypocrisy of the social class of English country squires.

Sister Mary Eulalia, RSM was a Catholic nun of the Sisters of Mercy of the Americas. Their mission is to serve the poor and needy as teachers, nurses, and in various community outreach programs. Sister Eulalia died in 1984.

James T. Fields (1817-81) was an esteemed American publisher. He helped to bring major authors such as Dickens, Tennyson, Hawthorne, and Harriet Beecher Stowe to the public. His humorous poem, "The Owl Critic" is also an enjoyable piece.

POET BIOGRAPHIES

Robert Frost, dubbed America's unofficial poet laureate, was the first poet to read at a presidential inauguration, reciting his poem "The Gift Outright" at the swearing in of John F. Kennedy. He achieved critical acclaim in his own lifetime (1874-1963), and received the Pulitzer Prize for Poetry four times. Frost typically combined solitary themes with images of nature, as in two of his beloved poems "Stopping by Woods on a Snowy Evening" and "The Road Not Taken."

James Henry Leigh Hunt (1784-1859) was a British poet, drama critic, editor, and essayist whose radical political views not only led him into camaraderie with other poet/reformers such as Percy Bysshe Shelley and Lord Byron, but also into prison. He penned the charming "Jenny Kissed Me," and his other well-loved poem is "Abou Ben Adhem," which according to research seems to have been memorized by countless grade school children prior to the 1960's. Enjoy!

The very first poem **Felicia Hemans** (1793-1835) wrote attracted the attention of Percy Bysshe Shelley. During her life fellow poets such as Wordsworth and Sir Walter Scott appreciated her writings; women were her most avid fans, however. Hemans raised five sons, produced plays and also composed Welsh folk songs. "Casabianca" is her chief claim to fame.

Oliver Herford (1863-1935) was a stand-up comedian, wrote children's poetry, illustrated, and published cartoons; he came from a large family of authors and artists. His friends nicknamed him "Peter Pan" because of his innocent, quick humor. Herford described a pest as "a man who can talk like an encyclopedia and does." Other funny poems for the young at heart include his "The Chimpanzee" and "The Hippopotamus."

Amazingly, nineteenth century American essayist, poet, novelist, and medical journalist **Oliver Wendell Holmes** achieved his literary prowess while chairing the Dartmouth and Harvard Anatomy and Physiology Departments from 1838 to 1892. His prose and poetry are celebrated as witty, brilliant, youthful, and original. He also wrote "Old Ironsides" and "The Last Leaf."

As a girl, **Mary Howitt** (1799-1888) was tutored at her home in England. She grew up in a loving family as evidenced by her poem entitled "The Clock is on the Stroke of Six," in which children eagerly await their father's arrival home from work. Howitt translated some of the stories of Hans Christian Andersen into German and joint authored several histories with her husband William Howitt.

"Trees" is **Alfred Joyce Kilmer**'s most famous poem. This American writer died in battle in France in 1918.

Benjamin Franklin King (1857-94) is a lesser known American poet and journalist. He was born in Michigan, raised a family in Chicago, and gave public readings. A collection of his children's poetry can be found in *Ben King's Verse*, 1894.

Edward Lear (1812-88) wrote limericks, you say? Nonsense!

POET BIOGRAPHIES

American author **William Ellery Leonard** (1876-1944) wrote many books, an autobiography, and several poetry collections. His translations of the epic poems *Beowulf* and *De Rerum Natura* (*On the Nature of Things*) by Roman philosopher Lucretius (50 B.C.) are considered his noteworthy achievements.

The poetry of **Henry Wadsworth Longfellow** (1807-1882) enjoyed large readership in its day because of its romantic treatment of simple stories, as for example in "The Village Blacksmith." He has been called the most popular American poet of the nineteenth century. Other celebrated works are "The Song of Hiawatha" and "The Midnight Ride of Paul Revere."

When he was a boy, **John Masefield** went to sea. After he published two volumes about his watery adventures, he was nicknamed "Poet of the Sea." In addition to poems like "Sea Fever," he is also remembered for his fine plays and novels. Masefield was Poet Laureate of England from 1930 until his death in 1967.

Sitting on the back step of an ambulance, anguished Canadian doctor **John McCrae** put down the words of the haunting poem "In Flanders Fields" after treating injured soldiers in Belgium during World War I. The wild poppies to which he referred blossomed on the grisly battlefields of the Western Front where no other plants would grow.

Some students of literature may find the life and works of **Hughes Mearns** (1875-1965) quite interesting. This influential American was the first educator to teach creative writing as a subject in its own right, the goal of which was to foster the emotional, spiritual, and intellectual growth of students. He penned his most famous piece "The Little Man Who Wasn't There," also known as "Antigonish," when he was twenty-four.

Another American author **George Perkins Morris** (1802-64) is primarily remembered as a poet. He also edited a magazine and composed hymns, such as the prayerful "Searcher of Hearts, from Mine Erase."

One of his biographers pronounced **Herman Melville** (1819-91) the greatest imaginative writer America had produced. *Moby Dick* was his masterful whale tale.

Ogden Nash (1902-71) was internationally famous as an author of extremely clever and amusing poems. Nash utilized the element of surprise, absurd plays on words, and newly invented words; persons of all ages have enjoyed his work. Despite all the silliness, however, Nash had a gift for touching upon the truths of the human experience.

William Brighty Rands (1823-82) contributed to English periodicals and published several volumes of children's poetry. "Great, Wide, Beautiful, Wonderful World" is another of his well-known poems.

Grantland Rice (1880-1954) is commonly acknowledged as the greatest American sportswriter. He coined the phrase "It's not whether you win or lose, it's how you play the

Poet Biographies

game" and nicknamed the "Four Horsemen of Notre Dame." He authored many books about sports. Often inserting his own poetry into his columns, Rice wrote "Game Called" upon the death of Babe Ruth.

Billy Rose (1899-1966) was a famous American showman. He sang, composed, and produced lavish musical plays. Rose married the Vaudeville comedienne Fanny Brice and composed the song "It's Only a Paper Moon."

Her father, Gabbriele Rossetti and brother Dante, also poets, were influential in **Christina Rossetti**'s success as a writer. Because she was a devout Christian, many of her poems are religious in nature. The poem "My Gift" is a stanza from "A Christmas Carol" which was set to music. She lived from 1830 to 1894 in London.

Internationally acclaimed author-poet **Carl Sandburg** (1878-1967) was the son of Swedish immigrants who settled in Illinois. After a college professor encouraged Sandburg to write, he became a journalist. He was awarded the Pulitzer Prize for his four-volume biography *Abraham Lincoln: The War Years*; he won a second time for *Complete Poems*. Sandburg is beloved for his free verse and down-to-earth words about the geography and the experience of the common people of America.

The author **Sir Walter Scott** (1771-1832) was a famous son of Edinburgh, Scotland where he grew up learning the ancient stories of his country. He employed this oral tradition in his lengthy narrative poems such as "The Lady of the Lake" and in his novels such as *Ivanhoe*.

William Shakespeare is the most widely studied British writer of all time. He lived from 1564-to 1616 during the reign of Queen Elizabeth I. "The Bard" penned many poems, and his matchless plays include comedies, dark histories like *Richard III*, and timeless tragedies such as *Hamlet* and *Romeo and Juliet*.

The famous Southern poet **Edward Rowland Sill**, better known by the pseudonym Sidney Lanier (1842-1881), grew up in Georgia. Although he was captured and confined for five months in a squalid Union Army prison, he went on to lecture at a university, author a fiction series for boys, and compose many remarkably optimistic, faith-filled poems such as "The Symphony" and his masterpiece, "Sunrise." Coming from a long line of gifted musicians, Lanier was acclaimed as a musical genius on the flute. Unfortunately, he died at the age of thirty-nine. In a letter he wrote, "…a thousand songs are singing in my heart that will certainly kill me if I do not utter them soon."

Robert Louis Stevenson was a Scottish poet, novelist, and essayist who lived from 1850 to 1894. This master storyteller initially gained fame with the swashbuckling adventure *Treasure Island*. His novel of mystery and murder, *The Strange Case of Dr. Jekyll and Mr. Hyde* has been adapted for the screen twenty times. However he is equally well known for his 1885 volume of poetry for children, *A Child's Garden of Verses*.

Literary critics throughout the years have both lauded the works of Lord **Alfred Tennyson** (1809-92) as philosophically important and decried them as sentimental and self-involved.

Poet Biographies

Nevertheless he is currently regarded as one of the great British poets. His major achievements are "In Memoriam," "Charge of the Light Brigade," and "Ulysses."

The American author **Ernest L. Thayer** (1863-1940) was a quiet, retiring man who wrote humor columns in the *San Francisco Examiner* newspaper for his Harvard classmate William Randolph Hearst. After he created "Casey at the Bat," he never submitted any other poem for publication.

New York born **Louis Untermeyer** (1885-1977) is appreciated for the writing of his own poetry as well as for the gathering of other poets' verses into valuable, satisfying compendia such as *This Singing World* and *Selected Poems and Parodies*.

"The hand that rocks the cradle is the hand that rules the world," wrote **W.R Wallace** (1819-81) in praise of motherhood. Although he is not much remembered today, his patriotic poems such as "The Liberty Bell" and "Last Words of Washington" were inspirational to Union soldiers during the Civil War.

Myra Brooks Welch's masterpiece was "The Touch of the Master's Hand." She is called "The Poet with the Singing Soul." Welch came from a family of musicians and was an organist until she became challenged by severe arthritis. No longer able to play, she typed out her poetry with the eraser ends of two pencils, one in each hand.

Carolyn Wells (1869-1942) was an American poet and anthologist. In *Such Nonsense: An Anthology*, she penned especially comical, satirical poetry.

Although **Walt Whitman**'s (1819-92) poems received mixed criticism by his contemporaries, he is an honored American writer. Primarily self-taught, he became a printer's apprentice at age eleven. By age sixteen he was helping to support his family as an editor and freelance writer. The poem "Leaves of Grass" was his life's work.

Mary Fabyan Windeatt's biographies of saints such as Benedict, Thomas Aquinas, and Catherine of Siena are currently best sellers in the juvenile non-fiction genre. She lived from 1811 to 1873 in England. Curiously, historians have more to report about her colorful father and her husband than about the genuinely talented member of the family—writer Mary.

During his day American songwriter **Henry Clay Work** (1832-84) was equally as popular as fellow Civil War composer Stephen Foster. Work wrote some one hundred songs. "Grandfather's Clock" sold almost one million copies when the sheet music was published.

Winner of the 1923 Nobel Prize for Literature, **William Butler Yeats** (1819-1939) is recognized as one of the greatest poets of the twentieth century. Irish born, he drew inspiration from the folklore of his country. He also wrote plays and was a senator and cultural leader. Two of his other famous fantasy-like poems are "The Everlasting Voices" and "When You Are Old."

BIBLIOGRAPHY OF ANTHOLOGIES

A Treasury of the World's Best-Loved Poems. New York: Avenel Books, 1931.

Berquist, Laura M. *The Harp and Laurel Wreath.* San Francisco, CA: Ignatius Press, 1999.

Bennett, William J., ed. *The Moral Compass—Stories for a Life's Journey.* New York: Simon & Schuster, 1995.

Bennett, William J., ed. *The Book of Virtues—A Treasury of Great Moral Stories,* New York: Simon & Schuster, 1993.

Felleman, Hazel, ed. *The Best-Loved Poems of the American People,* New York: Doubleday, 1936.

The Editorial Board of the University Society, eds. *The Home University Bookshelf Vol. V Famous Stories and Verse,* New York: The University Society, 1927.

Lear, Edward. *A Book of Nonsense.* New York: Alfred A. Knopf, Inc., 1992

Bloom, Harold, ed. *Stories and Poems for Extremely Intelligent Children of All Ages.* New York: Scribner, 2001.

Blishen, Edward, ed. *Oxford Book of Poetry for Children,* New York: Peter Bedrick Books, 1984.

Ferris, Helen, ed. *Favorite Poems Old and New,* New York: Doubleday & Company, Inc., 1957.

Hohn, Max T., ed. *Stories in Verse,* Indiana: The Bobbs-Merrill Company, Inc., 1978.

Carman, Bliss, ed. *The Oxford Book of American Verse,* U. S.: Oxford University Press, 1927.

Copeland, Lewis and Lamm, Lawrence W., eds. *The World's Great Speeches,* New York: Dover Publications, 1973.